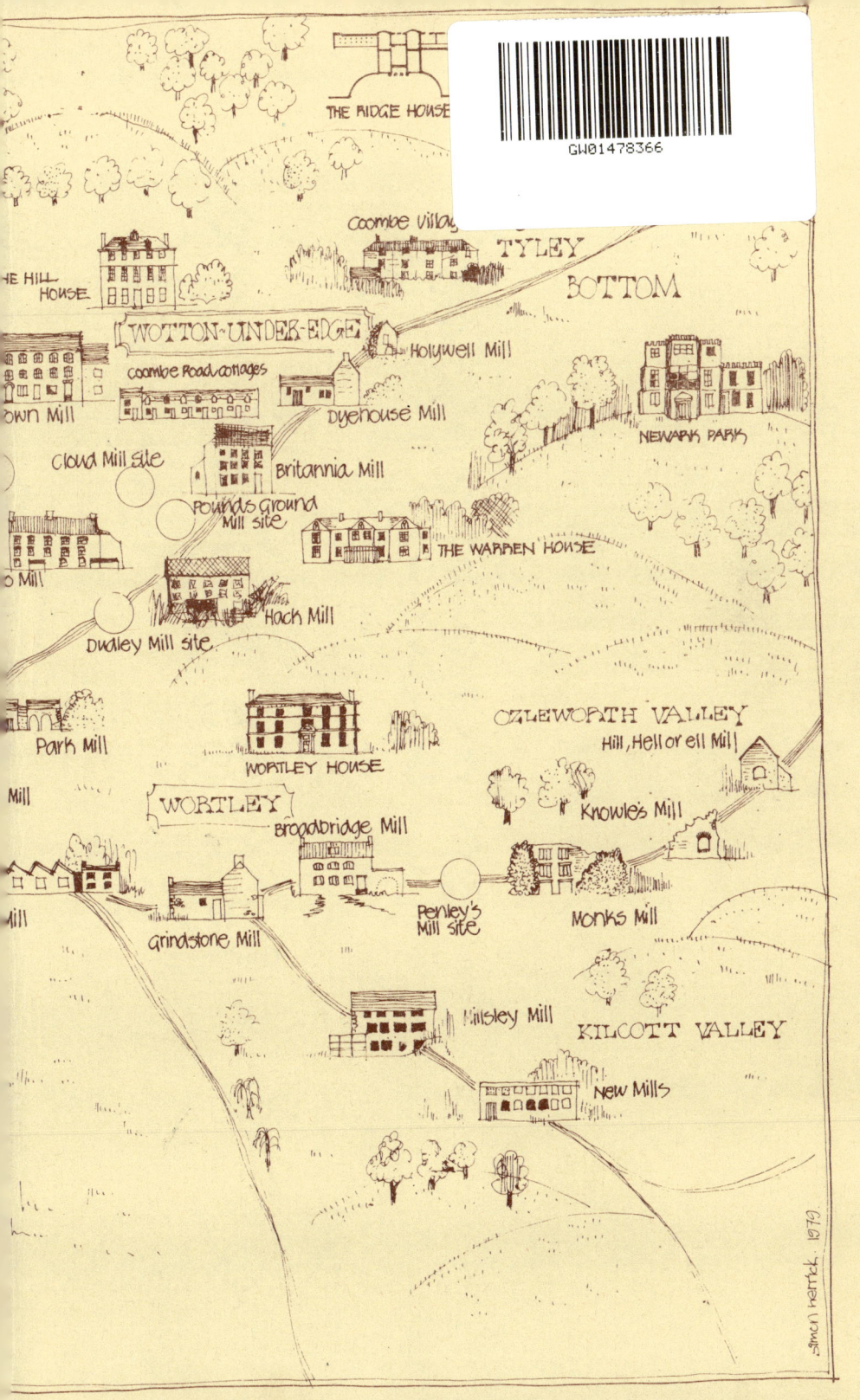

Jack. Christmas 1979.

Under the Hill

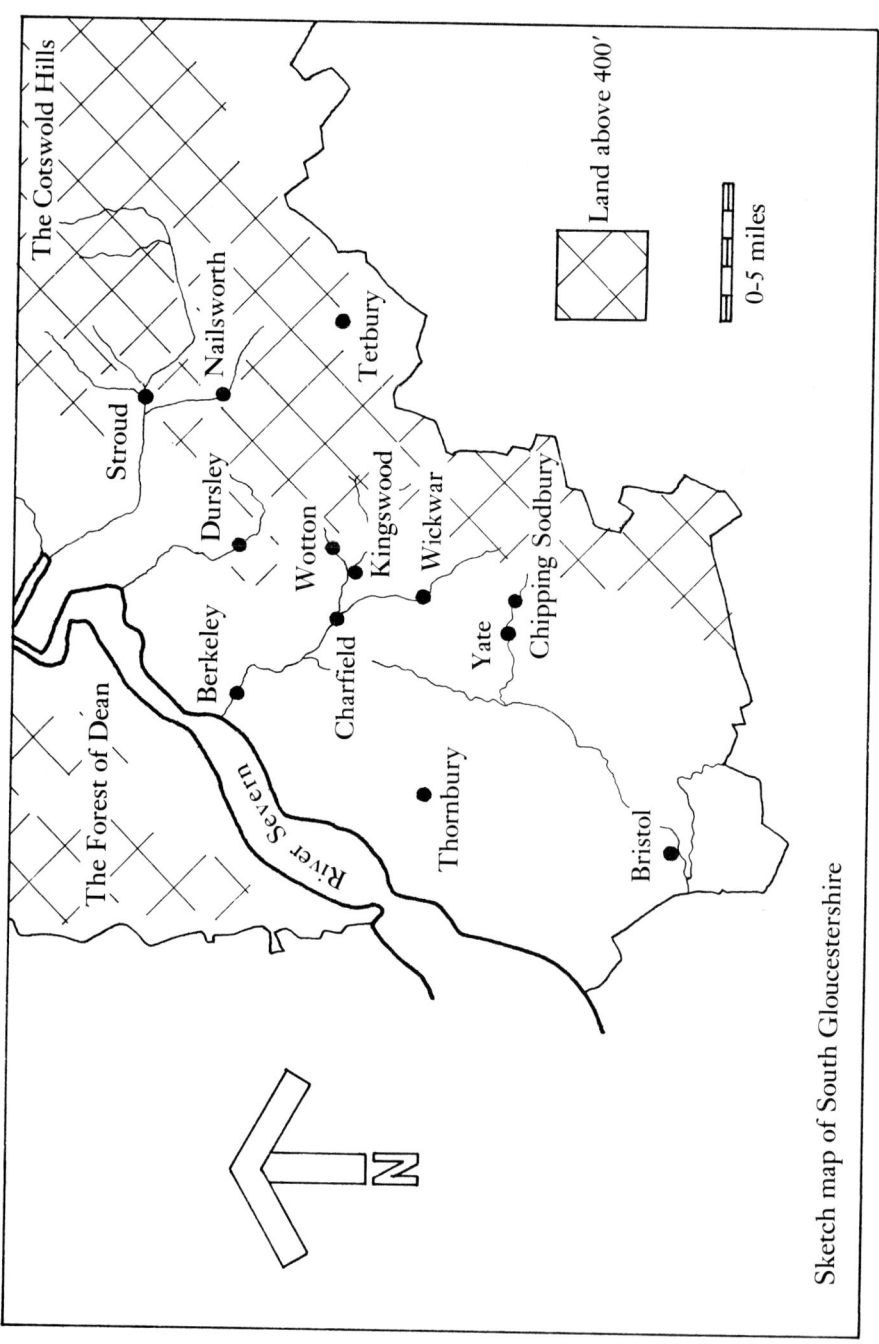

Sketch map of South Gloucestershire

Under the Hill

Simon Herrick

First published 1979 by
Alan Sutton Publishing Limited
17a Brunswick Road
Gloucester GL1 1HG

Copyright © Simon Herrick 1979

All rights reserved. No part of this publication may be reproduced, stored in a retrieval system, or transmitted, in any form or by any means, electronic, mechanical photocopying, recording or otherwise, without the prior permission of the Publisher.

ISBN 0 904387 36 4

British Library Cataloguing in Publication Data

Herrick, Simon
   Under the hill.
   1. Textile factories - England - Wotton-under-Edge
   2. Wotton-under-Edge, Eng. - Buildings
   3. Wool trade and industry - England - Wotton-under-Edge - History
   I. Title
   725'.4   NA6410

Typesetting and origination
by Alan Sutton Publishing Limited
Set Janson 11/13
Printed in Great Britain by
Redwood Burn Limited
Trowbridge & Esher

Under the Hill

Simon Herrick

ALAN SUTTON
1979

First published 1979 by
Alan Sutton Publishing Limited
17a Brunswick Road
Gloucester GL1 1HG

Copyright © Simon Herrick 1979

All rights reserved. No part of this publication may be reproduced, stored in a retrieval system, or transmitted, in any form or by any means, electronic, mechanical photocopying, recording or otherwise, without the prior permission of the Publisher.

ISBN 0 904387 36 4

British Library Cataloguing in Publication Data

Herrick, Simon
   Under the hill.
   1. Textile factories - England - Wotton-under-Edge
   2. Wotton-under-Edge, Eng. - Buildings
   3. Wool trade and industry - England - Wotton-under-Edge - History
   I. Title
   725'.4   NA6410

Typesetting and origination
by Alan Sutton Publishing Limited
Set Janson 11/13
Printed in Great Britain by
Redwood Burn Limited
Trowbridge & Esher

Contents

Illustrations .... Page	6
Acknowledgements	9
Introduction	11
1. The Woollen Cloth Industry	13
2. Energy Sources	25
3. The Nineteenth Century	35
4. Mills	47
5. Cottages	93
6. Houses	99
In Conclusion	123
Appendix I Berthold Lubetkin	125
Appendix II Aubrey Beardsley	127
Appendix III George Stanley Repton	130
Bibliography	133
Index	135

Illustrations

Sketch Map of South Gloucestershire. .... Frontispiece
The Shearmans Arms .... Page 22
Diagram of water wheel types 27
Diagram of mill placements 28
Sluice gates at Penley's Mill 34
Population of Wotton Civic Parish
during the nineteenth century 42
Hillesley Mill, east front 49
Hillesley Mill, an uninspired conversion 49
Alderley New Mills c.1900 50
Alderley New Mills 50
Hill, Hell or Ell Mill 52
The Ozleworth Valley 52
Knowles Mill c.1940 53
The ruins of Knowles Mill 53
Monks Mill c.1880 55
Water inlet at Monks Mill, showing
rubbed stonework arch detail 55
Ivy and Monks Mill 56
Flat arch detail at Monks Mill 56
Broadbridge Mill (conversion
by Berthold Lubetkin) east 59

Broadbridge Mill (conversion by Berthold Lubetkin) west	59
Grindstone Mill	60
Nind Mill c.1910	62
Nind Mill	63
Walk Mill and later Mill House	65
Park Mill, held together with ivy	65
Detail of Park Mill warehouse	66
Park Mill warehouse	66
Kingswood Abbey Gatehouse	70
Abbey Mill cottages	70
Fire at Abbey Mill, 1898	71
Much changed Abbey Mill	71
Langford Mill	73
New Mill	75
Converted wool drying stove at New Mill	76
The earliest (1812) of the Charfield Mills	78
The Charfield Mills	79
Date block on Charfield Mill	79
Huntingford Mill	82
Holywell or Strange's Mill remains	82
Dyehouse Mill and mill house	84
Britannia Mill as part of Neal's Mill site	84
The Steep Mill	86
Waterloo Mill	88
Date block on Waterloo Mill	88
Old Town Mill	90
Hack Mill	90
Tyley Bottom	92
Weaving cottages at Coombe village (south side)	94
Weaving cottages in Coombe village (north side)	94
Weaving cottages at Coombe village	95
Weaving terrace on Coombe road	95
Plan of weaving cottage in Bradley Green	97
Bradley Green weaving cottages	98

Newark Park 101
Newark Park showing Wyatt's
porch on the south front 101
Newark Park, present entrance and Great Dane 102
Newark Park, Solway's two-storey extension 102
Under the Hill, south front 106
Under the Hill 110
The Warren House 114
The Ridge, entrance facade c.1925 120
The Ridge, garden facade c.1925 120
The Ridge, from a sale notice 122
Under the Hill gateway 129

Acknowledgements

Bob Hewish must lead my list of grateful acknowledgements, the photographs speak for themselves, but those we adopted for publication represent a small proportion of some three hundred which were taken. I thank him for his consistent co-operation, despite some most tedious episodes — often caused by bad weather, deep mud, high fences or a frustrating day at the Gloucester Record Office. When I felt like giving up and forgetting the whole venture, Bob provided the encouragement which otherwise was usually lacking.

Research for *Under the Hill* started in 1971 under the close direction of Dr Roy Douglas in the Department of Humanities and Social Sciences at Surrey University. Work continued with advice and help from Jim Thompson and my tutor, Joe Holyoake, at Birmingham School of Architecture. Criticism by Dr. Jennifer Tann of Aston Universtiy and by Dr R Perry (local historian) has been very much appreciated, and was totally indispensable. I convey additional thanks to Dr Tann for allowing me to use her work on the Boulton and Watt papers.

I am most grateful to those people who allowed us to look at their mills or houses, or helped in other ways. Although it is impossible to list them all, I especially thank Bob Parsons of Newark Park; Robert Chidlaw for his help with Newark

Park and his permission to reproduce the sale notice of The Ridge: Mr and Mrs Lawrence of The Warren; Mr and Mrs Foster of Under the Hill; Mr Kirkham of Park Mill Farm; the people who allowed me to survey their cottages at Bradley Green; Mr Chappell of New Mill Farm; Mr Donald Emes who willingly provided the prints from which plates were prepared; John Harris at the RIBA drawings collection, who was patiently helpful with work on the Ridge; the staff at the Gloucester Record Office and the Gloucester City Library. Finally, Shire Publications Ltd., for permission to reproduce the illustrations on pages 27 and 28.

Simon Herrick

Author's Note

Wherever possible, I obtained permission from the respective owners or caretakers to visit the buildings featured in this book. I strongly emphasise that all these buildings, although accessible, are certainly not open to the public, and I therefore suggest that intending visitors should obtain similar permission. Once that permission has been obtained, then any close inspection of a building which is in a potentially dangerous condition is of course entirely at one's own risk.

Introduction

The buildings of the woollen cloth industry in Wotton-under-Edge and its neighbouring villages of Charfield, Kingswood and Wortley, form an epitaph to the trade which was the backbone of local prosperity for five hundred years. It was the principal source of employment; it was the principal generator of wealth; and ultimately, with the decline during the nineteenth century, it was the principal agent of poverty and starvation. The mills, workers' cottages and clothiers' houses, by their varied nature, provide examples both of good, unconscious building and fine, deliberate architecture. Inevitably and sadly several distinguished buildings have been either totally demolished or stand as nonchalent and decayed ruins which, as small consolation, perhaps allow a glimpse of a few eroded details or merely act as crumbling support for parasitic weeds and ivy. The destroyed buildings were of great importance to local industrial and domestic architectural history but worse, one or two were of national significance.

CHAPTER 1

The Woollen Cloth Industry

Wotton-under-Edge is a small Gloucestershire town, pleasantly situated on the south western edge of the Cotswold Hills, some twenty miles from Bristol to the south and Gloucester to the north; overlooking the Berkeley vale to the River Severn and, on a clear day, Wales beyond. Prehistoric and Roman remains suggest very early settlements, but the first recorded mention of the site, *Wudetun* (village in the wood), occurs in a Saxon manuscript of 940. In the Domesday Book of 1086 the name underwent Norman distortion and *Vutune* is described as a hamlet in the Royal Manor of Berkeley of "fifteen hides and a half yard land". The addition of 'under-Edge' appeared in some form in the fourteenth century and there have been several variations, including 'undyrheg', 'under-Hegge', 'underedge', and 'underidge'.

The disadvantages of remoteness, incurred through the problems of communication across clay vales and through steep-sided valleys, were offset by the capitalization of natural advantages which allowed the woollen cloth industry to become established.

During the thirteenth century, Wotton was slowly evolving into one of the important woollen cloth manufacturing centres of Gloucestershire, and was a market town as early as 1252.

Wool

The supply of Cotswold wool locally was vitally important for the early development of the industry, and the wool was used for coarser cloth. However, with specialisation in the production of fine broadcloth, imported Spanish Merino wool had largely superseded local wool by the end of the seventeenth century. Although Cotswold wool was being used for coarse cloth until the middle of the eighteenth century, its use was continually diminishing and, when sold at the Tetbury and Cirencester markets, much of it was destined for Yorkshire worsted cloth manufacture. Changes in the metabolism of Cotswold sheep due to cross-breeding, caused the bulk of the animal to increase; making the wool coarser and, by the end of the nineteenth century, suitable only for army blankets. Other English wools used in Gloucestershire included those from Hereford, Ross and Leicester and, during the nineteenth century, German, Australian and South African wools were being imported.

Water

The factor which above all determined the location of cloth mills was the existence and accessibility of fast flowing streams. These derive locally from springs which emerge between the strata of Cotswold sand and upper lias clay and between middle and lower lias clays. During the thirteenth and fourteenth centuries, the process of fulling cloth underwent mechanisation by the adaption of water powered wheels used in corn grinding. From at least the eleventh century, corn mills were sited along local streams to serve the agricultural community. Hence, several corn mills became fulling mills and it was the majority of these already established fulling mill sites which became the focus for expansion and factory development during the late eighteenth and early nineteenth centuries. Water-powered fulling superseded the archaic method of 'walking' a cloth, and indeed, the technological transition was so significant, in terms of the distribution of the cloth industry and the production of cloth, that it has been referred to as 'an early industrial revolution'. Water was a source of energy, and was also essential for washing and dyeing cloth, and several mills higher in the Coombe Valley became dyeworks, using water that was unpolluted by town waste, and whose temporary hardness could be easily removed by heat.

Fuller's Earth

Fuller's earth is a clay which lies locally between the strata of greater and inferior oolitic limestones. It was dug locally and used as a detergent in the process of 'scouring' or cleansing a cloth.

Teazels

Teazels are a type of thistle but more refined, and were essential for the roughing and mozing processes, (which involved raising the nap of a cloth into a pile, ready for shearing to a close surface). The quality and cultivation of teazels was critical and selection required care and experience. Suitable teazels were grown on richer clay soils around Cromhall, Filton and Almondsbury.

Organic Dyes

Several organic dyes were locally available in abundance and were of economic importance until the eighteenth century. Common examples included woad, which was used for a blue background dye and weld (or dyer's weed), which, when mixed with alum (potassium aluminium sulphate), yielded controllable shades of yellow. During the eighteenth century these dyestuffs were largely superseded by foreign imports, which in turn gave way to coal-based dyes (accidently discovered by Perkins in 1856.)

Bristol

Gloucestershire cloth was being exported through Bristol from at least the early fourteenth century and the city continued a dual role as port and financial centre. Although local agriculture provided investment capital during the initial stages of the cloth industry, it seems that in the fifteenth and sixteenth centuries this was provided by Bristol merchants. In the sixteenth and seventeenth centuries, dyestuffs were purchased mainly from Bristol markets. By the eighteenth century, most Gloucestershire cloth was sold at Blackwell Hall in London but, during the seventeenth, eighteenth and nineteenth centuries, most raw Spanish Merino wool was imported through Bristol.

Wotton-under-Edge became a woollen cloth manufacturing town because it was well positioned geographically and geologically and took full advantage of its indigenous resources. These characteristics which were not unique, of course, were shared by Dursley, Nailsworth and Stroud. Together, these centres formed the basis of the Gloucestershire cloth industry. By the end of the eighteenth century, Wotton's share in that industry (in terms of the number of mills, cloth production and relative population) amounted to about fifteen per cent, whilst that of the larger towns of Stroud and Nailsworth together, amounted to approximately sixty-five per cent.

The Processes in the Production of Woollen Cloth

By 1840, nearly thirty separate processes in the manufacture of cloth could be identified and grouped into four categories: preparing raw rool for spinning; spinning clean, fine wool into yarn; weaving yarn into cloth; and finishing cloth to a standard suitable for marketing. From opening and sorting one pack of wool to the final pressing of finished cloth made from that pack would have taken on average about two weeks. Some processes, although always effective, may well appear to have been rather haphazard and unsophisticated, whilst others, like dyeing and weaving, required considerable experience and skill.

I PREPARING THE WOOL

1. **Sorting.** New packs (usually 240 lbs) of raw wool were handsorted by skilled men and boys who were responsible for choosing wools to suit various cloths.

2. **Scouring.** Wool was cleaned of grease by immersing it into a warm, heady mixture of soap and stale human urine (a source of ammonia and colloquially and politely known as 'seg') which was collected in large vats on a sort of public subscription basis in Wotton. After five hours the wool was taken out of scouring tanks and put into wire baskets to be 'swilled' in a stream.

3. **Dyeing.** If a cloth was to be *wool-dyed*, the wool was then dyed, but if *piece-dyed*, the woven cloth itself was dyed later. Only larger mills had their own dyehouses, for example, Nind Mills and New Mills at Kingswood. Smaller mills depended either on those or on public dyers. Strange's Mill in Holywell and Dyehouse Mill in Coombe, both became dyeworks during the nineteenth century.

4. **Twillying.** A rotating spiked cylinder called *the Devil* next disentangled the woollen fibres and removed any dust or dye particles. During the early nineteenth century this process had been mechanised but previously had been done by hand-combing.

5. **Beating and Picking.** The wool was beaten with wooden poles and placed on a wire screen to be manually patted so that any remaining dirt particles fell through.

6. **Oiling.** Fine Galipoli oil was used to oil the wool.
7. **Scribbling.** Woollen fibres were further disentangled by passing them between fast revolving cylinders. This process was mechanised by the end of the eighteenth century and adapted initially to animal or water powered systems and later to steam power.
8. **Carding.** The scribbled wool resembled a very fine, thin fleece which was transferred to a carding machine. This in effect was similar to a scribbling machine but was fitted with cards. Carding was mechanised at about the same time as scribbling and was the final process of wool preparation, enabling the wool to be spun into yarn.

II SPINNING

Wool emerged from the carding machines in rolls and was spun into *warp yarn* (the longitudinal thread) and *abb yarn* (the weft, or transverse thread which was usually coarser than the warp yarn). The coarser abb yarn was spun on a *billy* or *jack* in a process called *slubbing*. The finer warp yarn was spun on a Spinning *jenny* and later a Spinning *mule*. Until the end of the eighteenth century, spinning had always been a cottage industry, serving as the staple occupation of many local women and children using traditional spinning wheels: "the yarn was distributed to various persons at their own dwellings, the families and farm servants used to spin during the evening and the manufacturers used to employ . . . spinning-house-men, to meet the isolated spinners at various rendezvous for miles around the county to select, fortnightly, the spun yarn". But with the mechanisation of spinning by the introduction of Spinning Jennies, spinners were brought into mills and thus underwent the transition from cottage to factory. Hargreave's Spinning Jenny was patented in 1770 for use in the cotton industry. Its adaptation for woollen yarn and its introduction into Gloucestershire (about 1776) was met with violent opposition. Initially, the Jenny was manually operated, but with the later development of Arkwright's Water Frame, it was converted for water power. Crompton's Mule was invented in 1774, again for cotton, and it was a hybrid (hence *mule*) of the Jenny and Arkwright's Water Frame, and was suitable for water or steam power. It was introduced into Gloucestershire for spinning wool in about 1830, but its spread was slow; for instance, three local mills which were sold in the 1840's used only Spinning Jennies: Holywell Mill (November, 1841), Walk Mill in Kingswood (February, 1842) and Alderley New Mills (May, 1842). The spun yarn was reeled or wound into coils and the warp yarn was measured and cut to a length or chain (3 yards and 3 inches) before being sent to be woven into cloth.

III WEAVING

1. **Sizing.** Before the chain of yarn could be fixed or 'turned on' to a loom it had to be sized with a very dilute glue. Sizing was usually done in a Mill.

2. **Weaving.** The process of weaving on a hand loom is confusing to describe, but is similar to darning! Traditionally, the *outdoor* hand-loom weaver collected chains of spun yarn from the clothier who employed him, and wove the yarn into cloth at home. By about 1795 in Wotton, outdoor weaving represented the last of the processes of cloth manufacture which were based on the 'putting-out' or cottage system. Many cottages in Wotton probably housed looms, but some were specifically built as weaving cottages and examples of these are described later. The transistion to the factory system in this part of the industry was more vehemently opposed than any other and was to be the cause of hardship and, in some cases, violence.

The only significant improvement to the hand-loom was the Spring Shuttle which was a form of Kay's Flying Shuttle. The Flying Shuttle was invented in 1733 for cotton weaving, but it was not until about 1796 that the Spring Shuttle was introduced into Gloucestershire for woollen weaving. Before the Spring Shuttle, the shuttle carrying the weft had to be laboriously passed from one hand to the other. A weaver managed a narrow loom alone, but a broadloom required the assistance of a *journeyman*. The improvement enabled the shuttle to be passed from side to side with "force and facility", but displaced the need for journeymen. The Flying Shuttle meant that one man could do "more in ten hours than two used to do in twelve hours".

The later introduction of water and steam powered weaving gave rise to further unemployment, but apart from one power loom at Monks Mill mentioned in 1865, probably no others were locally introduced; it seems that clothiers of Wotton, Charfield and Kingswood were not prepared to invest in power weaving. Power looms in fact proved difficult to adapt to weaving fine woollen cloth and, although several Stroud and Nailsworth Mills housed some power looms in 1840, their spread was generally rather slow.

IV FINISHING CLOTH FOR THE WHOLESALE MARKET

1. **Scouring and washing.** The woven cloth was taken back to the Mill to be scoured, but this time with a pungent mixture of human urine and pigs' dung, and then washed with fuller's earth and water. Until about 1810, washing with fuller's earth was done as part of the fulling process, but later the process was carried out independently in a specially designed washing machine.

2. **Burling.** Any broken threads or dirt particles were picked out by hand.
3. **Fulling, felting or milling.** The cloth was saturated with soap or fuller's earth and water and subjected to the rise and fall of heavy stocks, felting it into a cloth of regular thickness. This process, of absolute importance, was carried out continuously for a minimum of twelve hours, and often as much as twenty-four or thirty-six hours. The ancient method of foot-treading, or *walking*, a cloth was superseded by waterpowered fulling mills and continued as such for centuries until it was adapted at the beginning of the nineteenth century for steam power.
4. **Roughing and mozing.** These processes involved raising the surface, or *nap*, of newly fulled cloth into a pile, or *dress*, and this was done with a rapidly revolving cylinder, or *gig-mill*, covered in teazel heads, brushing the nap of the cloth. If *gigging* was done in both directions, it was called *roughing*; if only in one, it was called *mozing*. Water-powered gig-mills were common in Gloucestershire by the middle of the seventeenth century. They were operated through a gearing system from fulling machinery.
5. **Shearing.** The raised pile of the cloth was next sheared to a close, smooth surface. Until the end of the eighteenth century, shearing had been done by hand-operated shears, but was then mechanised by use of a shearing frame. The frame was later superseded by a rotary cutting machine which was invented in 1825. Until shearing was mechanised, it was done by heavy, manually operated shears. The *shearmen* who did this job worked on a tightly closed-shop basis and carried specially issued tickets for identification and employment. Shearmen had to be strong and skilled and were "often drunk and disorderly"; they dictated

The Shearman's Arms.

when and how they worked, and, almost, how much they earned. They formed an exclusive and wealthy class of cloth-worker and, when they were displaced by mechanisation, many of them could afford to take up other trades, or make their own investments in the cloth industry. The *Shearman's Arms* pub in Wotton gains its name from these characters.

6. **Dyeing.** If the cloth had been made of white, undyed wool, then it was now dyed *in the piece*.

7. **Patent Boiling.** Adopted in about 1826, this was a method of giving the material a slight gloss by tightly rolling it around cylinders and immersing them into very hot water (180°F) for twenty-four hours.

8. **Drying.** The cloth was dried either in heated air stoves or on racks. The fields which were used for drying cloth on racks were conveniently close to mills and invariably called 'Rack Close'.

9. **Picking.** The cloth when dry was hung against daylight and picked, with tweezers, of any remaining particles or broken threads.

10. **Drawing.** After picking, the cloth was checked for any small holes which were carefully mended.

11. **Marking.** Each cloth was numbered and identified with the clothier's mark (if he had one) in white or yellow silk embroidery.

12. **Brushing.** Using equipment similar to a gig-mill, but fitted with bristles rather than teazels, the pile was very lightly brushed or mozed, giving the cloth its finished dressing.

13. **Pressing.** Finally, the cloth was folded, with *press papers* (which were made in Wotton at Hack Mill) placed between each fold, and then pressed between iron presses.

Before the late eighteenth century, the production of woollen cloth was based upon the *putting-out* system in which some processes of production were carried out as cottage industries: prepared wool was distributed to hand carders and spinners to be spun into yarn, which was then returned to the mill to be cut to 'chain' lengths and sized. The *out-door* weaver then collected yarn from the mill to be woven into cloth at home. The woven, but unfinished, cloth was then taken back to the mill to be finished. At that time, a streamside mill was primarily a finishing mill, housing water powered fulling and gigging machinery. However, during the late eighteenth century, carding and spinning processes were brought into mills and, as more mechanised processes were concentrated into mills, there came a need for extensions, or rebuilding on a grander, factory scale. Because looms took up a lot of valuable space and the factory system was more strongly opposed by unionised weavers, the change from cottage weaving to *loom-shop* weaving was much slower than that of other processes.

The transition to the factory system, with its associated concentrations of mechanised processes, occurred during the period 1810-1825, when nearly all the local mills were extended or totally rebuilt. The new buildings usually replaced small, two-storey, water powered fulling mills and were often of four or five storeys. Although they may have been different in size and activity from their predecessors, they still depended for their functioning on their supply of energy, and it is a consideration of this to which we next turn.

CHAPTER 2

Energy Sources

Although some use of animal power had been made in small workshops, the overwhelming majority of woollen cloth mills were dependent upon water power and therefore had been sited near streams. It was not until the nineteenth century, with the advent of steam power, that this pattern changed. A more detailed discussion of the application of animal power, water power and steam power not only provides a deeper insight into the local woollen cloth industry, but also into the concept of "a mill".

Animal Power

A limited use of horses and oxen was made in the scribbling, carding and shearing processes, but because fulling required at least twelve hours of continuous effort, cloth from animal powered workshops was sent to be fulled at water powered fulling mills. Some animal wheels were horizontal, enabling more horses or oxen to be attached as required, whilst others were vertical and were worked by one animal treading within the wheel. An animal powered system was often used as a means to accumulate enough capital to invest in water or steam powered mills, and was especially suited to some farmers who held aspiration to clothier status. No examples of these workshops have been confirmed in Wotton, but there was one in Berkeley (at Oil Mill) in 1802 and one in Uley in 1815.

Water Power

Since the early development of water powered fulling mills, water remained the principal source of energy for mills until the nineteenth century, but even then, with the advent of steam power, some mills were designed solely for water power and some retained their water power to be worked in conjunction with steam power. A full appreciation of pre-nineteenth century Wotton-under-Edge as a water power town, self sufficient in industrial energy, is difficult to acquire because this indigenous energy system has long since been replaced by the national grid of a centralised, high technology society.

The kinetic energy of water flowing from a higher level to a lower level can be converted into mechanical energy by means of a water wheel. There are two basic types of water wheel (refer to the diagrams on page); the *overshot*, with water ducted over the circumference of the wheel, and the *undershot*, with water passing below. An overshot wheel is generally more efficient than an undershot wheel, but requires a higher head of water, perhaps between 10 and 30 feet, compared with 2 to 10 feet for an undershot wheel, depending on the size and design of the wheels. Overshot wheels are better suited to steep valleys and are more often found at sites in the Pennines or Scotland. However, a well designed *high breast* undershot wheel (the water meeting the wheel at about axle height) can be nearly as efficient as an overshot wheel, whilst using a lower head of water. On local stream sites with slight gradients, a high breast wheel, with suitable water courses and a reservoir to provide the head of water, would have been the theoretical choice; but a choice which was ultimately determined by the special characteristics of each particular site. Surviving

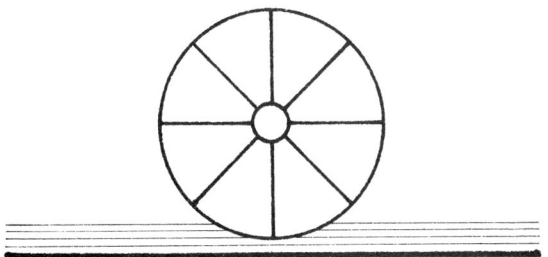

Simple undershot   mechanical efficiency 30%

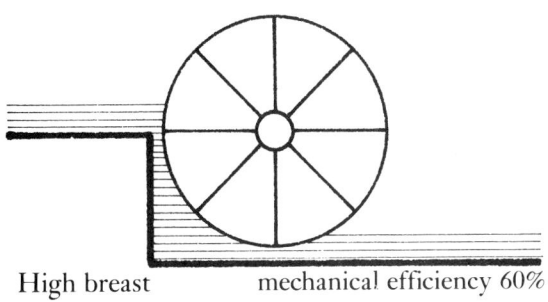

High breast   mechanical efficiency 60%

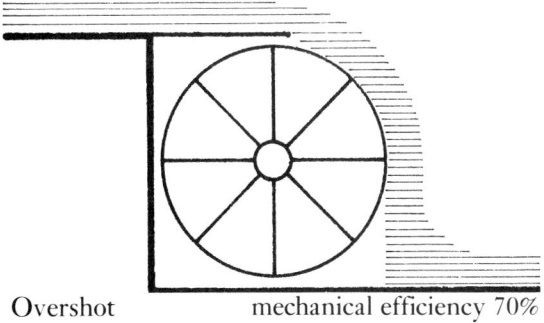

Overshot   mechanical efficiency 70%

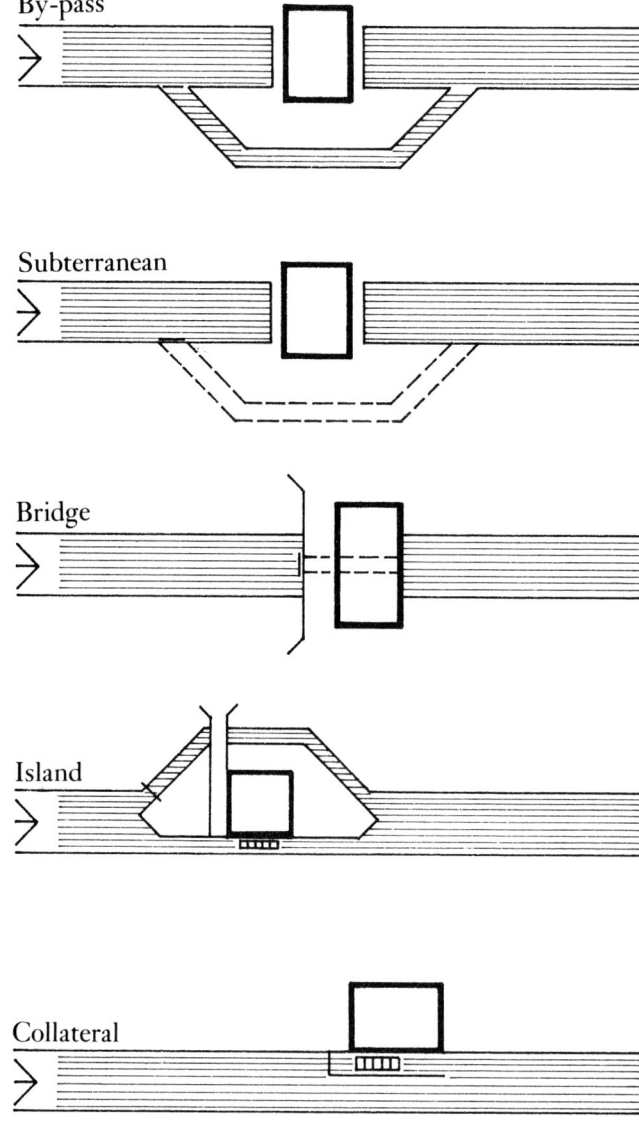

remains of civil engineering work at several mills illustrate that clothiers and their millwrights were extremely ingenious water technologists, with an acute ability to assess sites in order to exploit the optimum water power available from them. During the eighteenth century the power requirements of a mill (perhaps the size of Broadbridge Mill in Wortley) operating scribbling, carding, gigging and fulling machinery, would have amounted to approximately 10 horse power, and this could be satisfied by one well designed and constructed high breast wheel about 12 feet in diameter. In larger mills or factories of the nineteenth century, the number and size of wheels were increased to meet greater power requirements of larger scale mechanisation and production. Where mills were not crowded together, mill ponds and associated water courses could be of considerable proportions, and this was especially the case at Hill Mill in the Ozleworth Valley, and New Mills and Nind Mills at Kingswood. New Mills housed five water wheels and generated an average of 45 horse power. Nind Mill was powered by at least five wheels, three of which were approximately 8 feet wide.

Bucket wheels gave rise to rather special problems of maintenance and efficiency and were more expensive than paddle wheels, which were an older form of water wheel technology, but were simpler and more generally preferred. In the late eighteenth century, the installation of a wooden paddle wheel and associated mill work may have cost about £50, but with the later adoption of cast iron wheels this cost would have increased further. The civil engineering work for a new cloth mill probably cost about £150 to £300; or less, where only minimal modification to existing watercourses was necessary in order to change a grist mill or simple fulling mill into a cloth mill. However, the work at Nind Mill, which had one of the largest mill ponds in Gloucestershire, may have cost as much as £1,200 in the early nineteenth century, but this scheme was an exception and is more comparable with the sites of northern cotton mills.

The various relations of mills to their streams, and ways of regulating the flow of water through them by diverting some of the flow via sluice gates, provide a simple means of identifying a standard mill type (page 28).*

The *collateral* and *island* arrangements are more typical of earlier unsophisticated grist mills with exposed water wheels. However, Langford Mill in Kingswood seems to be a collateral type, but with housed wheels. Monks Mill was an early grist mill and parts of it were built on a small island, but it was not of a pure island type. The earliest (1812) of the three Charfield Mills provides an obvious example of the *bridge* type of arrangement, with stream water flowing under the adjacent road and into the mill. The majority of local cloth mills of the late eighteenth and early nineteenth centuries, however, were built on the *by-pass* pattern, easily identifiable examples of which are Broadbridge Mill and Dyehouse Mill. Where physical or legal obstructions prevented the simple by-pass arrangement, a *subterranean* sluice tunnel may have been excavated, and there is an example of this at New Mills in Kingswood. Very often mills do not readily fall into an easily recognisable type and can well be a combination of two or more systems.

Steam Power

By the end of the eighteenth century, the ingenuity and proficiency of water power technology represented the culmination of generations of experience, but no matter how sophisticated a water power installation could be, it was ultimately dependent on the moods of the weather. Excesses of wet and dry weather could cause flooding on the one hand, or seriously underpower a mill on the other. Although

---

* These types have been identified by, among others, John Vince in *Watermills*, Shire Publications.

mill ponds and sluices were designed to minimise the effects of variations in water supplies, steam power provided a reliable means of supplementing these, and it was mainly for this reason that woollen cloth manufacturers began to take an interest in steam engines for their mills.

A steam engine povides a means of translating heat energy into motive power. Its empirical development during the seventeenth and eighteenth centuries was climaxed by Watt's Double-Acting Rotative Steam Engine, which was patented in 1782. The first Boulton and Watt engine to be installed in a textile mill of any type was erected in a cotton mill in Nottingham in 1785. It was during the 1790s that the Boulton and Watt factory in Soho, Birmingham, began to receive tentative enquiries from clothiers in the West of England woollen cloth counties of Somerset, Wiltshire and Gloucestershire. None of these enquiries actually resulted in an order until 1802, when the very first Boulton and Watt steam engine to be used in a West of England woollen cloth mill was installed in a mill in Wotton-under-Edge. The mill was the Steep Mill off Ludgate Hill. Unfortunately, this building, of major industrial archaeological importance, has been demolished. The engine was not used to supplement water power but to drive a mill totally independent of water power. This was a tremendously important innovation and establishes Wotton-under-Edge as a pioneering town of the Industrial Revolution.

The Watt patent expired in 1800, and although other makes of steam engine (Trevithick and Wolff, or Fenton, Murray and Wood, for example, were later bought by clothiers, it is almost certain that the Boulton and Watt engine in Wotton in 1802 was the first of any make of steam engine to be installed in a West of England cloth mill, making it one of the first in Britain to be used in the production of woollen cloth. This says much for the initiative and foresight of the firm, H. & G. Austin, who bought the engine, and the Austin family will be appearing again and again as key figures in the local cloth industry.

Other Gloucestershire clothiers, however, were slow to invest in steam power, and many held a stubborn faith in cheaper water power. In 1804, a Boulton and Watt engine of 20 horse power would have cost about £1,000, and the six horse power engine which the Austins bought, probably cost £600. Apart from the cost of the engine, an engine room and boiler-house would have accounted for another £300. As only small engines were required during the early nineteenth century, it is little wonder that when confronted with the high per-unit cost of steam engines, clothiers were hesitant to buy them when their needs could be adequately satisfied with water power. Nevertheless, further Boulton and Watt engines were bought for mills in Wotton: in 1808, William Strange of Strange's Mill in Holywell bought a small Boulton and Watt engine which was used to supplement water power at the site, but after having somewhat overrun the agreed credit period, Mr Strange only paid up when, in 1810, he was threatened with legal action. In 1815, Waterloo Mill was built by the Austins as a steam mill, but the engine was not a Boulton and Watt. In 1817, Old Town Mill was built for a twenty horse power steam engine, which again was not a Boulton and Watt. By this time Wotton had three mills which had been built for steam engines: Steep Mill, Waterloo Mill, and Old Town Mill. The building of these mills was stimulated by the advantage of being independent of water power, and because the existing stream sites were very expensive and already occupied.

In 1820, a small Trevithick steam engine may have been installed (as a supplementary power source) at Neals Mill, which stood near the present site of Britannia Mill, and then, in 1823, the Neal brothers bought a 20 horse power Boulton and Watt engine for the same mill, but they requested an extension of their credit period. Obviously great believers in the new energy, during 1825 they bought a 27 horse power engine and a 50 horse power engine, both of Boulton and Watt manufacture. In 1820, the Austins bought a 14 horse power Boulton and Watt engine, which was probably put into Hillsley Mill, and, in 1823, they bought a 32 horse power engine almost certainly destined for what was at that time the huge complex of Alderley New Mills in the Kilcott valley. Although one or two more steam engines filtered into Wotton, it is interesting to note that, at the better water power sites in the Ozleworth Valley and Kingswood, mills depended almost entirely on water power. By the 1830s, with the slow advent of powered spinning and weaving, the water power at these mills would have been inadequate for the latest machinery.

Despite the fact that Boulton and Watt engines were considerably more expensive than other types, they continued to hold much of the West of England market. This is partly attributable to the activities of their agent, George Haden, who was an excellent millwright and engineer, and whilst resident at Trowbridge in Wiltshire, he travelled extensively throughout the district during the 1820s and 1830s. Boulton and Watt engines were certainly reliable and were relatively economical in their consumption of coal. However, the enquiries from West of England clothiers about Boulton and Watt engines showed concern not only for the initial capital outlay, but also for rate of coal consumption. Enquiries from Yorkshire woollen cloth regions rarely mentioned coal consumption as a factor in making a decision to buy a steam engine. Gloucestershire clothiers bought their coal from the Forest of Dean and Staffordshire coalfields, and paid about £1. 0s. 0d. for each ton; much of the cost being for transport. In Yorkshire, coal was only one third of this price. The smallest Boulton and Watt engine, of 6 horse power, working for a twelve hour day, would have consumed about two tons of coal a week; and larger engines were much less economical to run. The price of coal may have accounted for only less than 1 per cent of the running costs of a mill, but that, plus maintenance costs and the initial capital investment, deterred many Gloucestershire clothiers from buying a steam engine. After all, fuel for a water powered mill was free.

Sluice gates at Penley's Mill.

CHAPTER 3

The Nineteenth Century

By the middle of the sixteenth century, Wotton-under-Edge had long been established as a "pratty Market Towne, welle occupyed withe Clothiars" and had "one faire longe strete, and is standithe clyvinge towards to rotes of an hill". In 1608, of just over 300 Wotton men who were considered suitable for military service, some fifty per cent were employed in the cloth industry and more than half of those were weavers. Agriculture accounted for twenty per cent of local employment, whilst various other trades (smiths, shopkeepers, carpenters and masons, for example) accounted for thirty per cent.

The Gloucestershire cloth industry as a whole was structured on a capitalist basis and relied heavily upon the mechanism of the putting-out system. During the middle of the seventeenth century, £300 was probably sufficient to buy an equipped finishing mill and perhaps an adjoining mill house, whereas by the middle of the eighteenth century this initial investment capital had almost doubled. The investment could pay handsome dividends; for instance, Jonathon Witchell of Wotton (who may have owned Holywell Mill and Dyehouse Mill, but certainly was an active entrepreneur — buying, selling and letting mills) died in 1701 and left £3,000, nearly half of which was circulating capital and the rest fixed capital. Successful weavers, of more the 'weaver — clothier' class, and shearmen who had accumulated enough capital to invest in their own businesses were often resented by already established clothiers, probably for social reasons, or because they undersold by producing poor quality cloth. However, wealthier novices were usually made most welcome by their neighbours who, in these cases, offered help and advice if it was requested. Success depended to a large degree upon keeping well informed as to the demands for various types and colours of cloth, and, because home and export markets were in fact so unpredictable, trade fluctuations had always been a haunting characteristic of woollen cloth industry. It was the lack of capital of smaller firms that led to several bankruptcies during recurrent trade depressions and, although credit extended by the cloth merchants of Blackwell Hall meant short-term respite, it eventually could lead to deeper debt and longer-term suffering.

Wotton-under-Edge entered the nineteenth century with an air of confidence and prosperity. There were nearly thirty woollen cloth mills fully operational, and the general optimism of the period was reflected by a growth in population during the first decade, which was double that of most other cloth towns. Wotton had become a leading producer of cassimer[1] cloth, whilst Kingswood was an important Spanish[2] cloth village. Nevertheless, there was considerable underlying industrial unrest, for which there were several reasons rather beyond parochial control. With the introduction of the Spinning Jenny and Flying Shuttle, the industry had suffered overproduction, and so was unable to absorb extra labour which had resulted from an influx of unemployed soldiers following the short-lived Peace of Amiens (between England and France in 1802). Furthermore, the situation was aggravated by high wheat prices[3] during the years 1801 to 1804, following a series of poor harvests.

Because so visually obvious as symbols and instruments of exploitation, perhaps the worst of all the threats to the local working population, was the gradual development of factory system mills which housed hand-looms. This heralded the beginning of the end of cottage weaving. The adoption of the Spring Shuttle, together with the weakening of the traditions of the putting-out system for weaving, seriously undermined the cohesion of the weaving fraternity. Journeymen, who were largely displaced by the Spring Shuttle, willingly accepted work in weaving factories or loom-shops. Master outdoor weavers, on the other hand, campaigned against loomshops by advocating legislation to limit the number of looms housed in any building to a maximum of two. The attitude of some of the weavers was actually rather ambivalent because several of them currently held more than two looms in their cottages. However, as an expression of apparent solidarity, they formed 'The Woollen Cloth Weavers Society', which was led by self-styled 'king of the weavers', Timothy Exell of North Nibley, and organised in Wotton by 'general' Joseph Wolfe, whose military status was of dubious authenticity, but whose intentions were geniune and noble. Through their efforts they were able to delay — but not prevent — the transition of weaving from cottage to factory: during the first few years of the nineteenth century, two workshops (possibly at Bear Street and Haw Street) in Wotton housed ten and eleven looms respectively; whilst one of the first large-scale installations in Gloucestershire was at New Mills in Alderley which housed twenty broadlooms in 1806.

The brief and strained period of Anglo-French détente was followed by the Napoleonic Wars (1803 to 1815) and an immediate stimulation in the demand for Gloucestershire uniform cloth. Expanding markets in India and new markets in China reinforced the demand for cloth, and these years were generally prosperous ones for Wotton. But in 1807,

Russia allied with the French. The Austins that year were left holding £15,000 worth of stock which had been destined for the Russian market. Although Napoleon's 'continental system' (a commercial blockade of England) was only partially successful, it was probably the main reason why the Austins' profits "remained low" for at least four years. Austins were not solely dependent on turbulent export markets, of course, and were probably manufacturing cassimere cloth for the home market: their profits for 1811 to 1812 were £16,000 and in 1813 were £10,000.

The second decade of the nineteenth century marked the beginning of a series of major building investments including Austins New Mill at Kingswood, about 1810, (and their Warren House shortly afterwards); the first of the three Charfield Mills, in 1812; Dudley Mill; extensions at Strange's Mill, in 1812; extensions and rebuilding at Nind Mill, in 1817; rebuilding at Walk Mill, about 1819; Langford Mill, in 1822 and Neals Mill which, in 1823, had been "lately erected". 1815 and 1817 also saw the building of the two steam mills — Waterloo Mill and Old Town Mill, which have been previously mentioned.

With the loss of the East India Company's monopoly of trade in India after 1812, and a further drop in demand for uniform cloth after the Napoleonic Wars, came corresponding falls in exports of cloth and, by 1819, the Austins were in deficit by £15,000 and had lost a further £7,000, by 1822.

The 1820s opened with further uncertainty in the cloth industry. In medium types of cloth there was increasing competition with Yorkshire, where worsteds manufacture was expanding to meet a demand for cheaper cloth from a growing national population, whilst Gloucestershire was generally concentrating on the production of super-fine broadcloth, which anachronistically served an exclusive and diminishing market. English cloth exporters had unsuccessfully attempted to re-enter the once lucrative Russian market and were also faced with extreme competition in Europe against high tariff-protected products, which was only partially compensated for by new markets in South America.

Meanwhile, serious trouble was brewing on the domestic front. Gloucestershire cloth had generally been improved by closer weaving and the extra work involved had not been rewarded by any wage increases; on the contrary, clothiers attempted to reduce the wages of their weavers, and this move was greeted by a series of illegal strikes. With the repeal of the Combination Acts in 1824, came the full emergence of the Woollen Cloth Weavers Society from behind its facade as a "union savings bank". According to Timothy Exell, it was in March and April of 1825 that "discontent began to show itself in every bosom; the union spread in every direction, and increased from 4,000 to 5,000 in a few days." On 28 April 1825, weavers stopped work in an attempt to raise low minimum wages and to equalize wages. On 4 May, the Chairman of the Clothiers Committee, Edward Sheppard (see The Ridge, below pp. 117-122) suggested a wage rate for his own weavers with which he hoped other clothiers would agree. Wotton clothiers did agree and a precarious industrial peace was re-established for seven months. The underselling of labour in an overstocked and often half-starved labour market was obviously very difficult for the union to control, and in November the Neal brothers in Wotton paid reduced wages to their weavers in the form of *truck*, or goods and food. For several days Wotton weavers stopped work and attended mass meetings in The Chipping in order to formulate some collective course of action. Work done by some dissenting weavers was seized and publicly burned, and their houses were mobbed. One such dissenter was Benjamin Fox, who was dragged to a tribunal meeting in The Swan Hotel and there threatened by Timothy Exell and Joseph Wolfe to the extent that he thought his "life was in danger." The climax to the whole affair was a march, on 24 November 1825, from The Chipping and through the streets to Edward and Thomas Neals' factory where, according to a witness, Edwin Derrett, the breaking of a window in the mill prompted Thomas Neal and his lackeys to fire at the defenceless crowd and hit sixteen unarmed men, women and children with musket shot.

The subsequent trial took place at The White Lion Inn and was presided over by Anthony Adey, JP. Dispensing swift justice, he granted bail to the men who fired the shots, but immediately imprisoned all the wounded. Timothy Excell got off comparatively lightly with a "discharge by proclamation" (a conditional discharge). When the court rose in the evening, the news of the proceedings filtered through the waiting crowds, who rushed to Neal's house and attacked it with stones and were only prevented from burning down the mill by two hundred special constables. Hopefully the tension had eased by the time a troop of the 12th Lancers rode into Wotton a few days later.

The Neal brothers may have tried to reduce wages in an effort to pay for the steam engines which they had bought at an almost fanatical rate, but in fact 1825 was a year of very serious general financial crisis, beginning with the industrial problems which lost some orders to Yorkshire and ending with the great 'panic' of December with the failure of several Gloucestershire banks. Adding to the problems of cloth manufacture, there was a massive increase in North American import tariffs and virtually an overnight collapse of South American markets, following the suspension of British loans for new republican governments. These culminating factors resulted in a sudden plunge into deep depression, and Wotton-under-Edge was particularly badly hit, with several bankruptcies following shortly after 1825. People in Wotton were soon to suffer extreme poverty. In the *Gloucester Journal* of 16 December 1826, a Bristol benevolent committee published a plea for financial aid for the unemployed of Wotton: "This parish contains between 5,000 and 6,000 inhabitants, 2,000 of whom are in such distress, that our funds are totally inadequate to their relief. It is really heart-rending to see the families, who were formerly decent, having nothing but rags to cover them, and entirely through want of employment. On entering the cottages we often find the children crying with cold and hunger, having only straw to lie upon, whilst the parents are reduced to such distress as to be utterly unable to alleviate their sufferings . . . ".

In 1828, Gloucestershire clothiers attempted to reduce weavers wages by 10 per cent. To oppose this the weavers formed a 'secret society' and again stopped work, but this time they were locked out by their employers, and when they eventually ran out of funds, were forced to accept work for any price that was offered. The action of 1828 was the last concerted effort made by weavers to secure themselves a fair wage. Their society was infiltrated by a Home Office spy, Francis Fagin, who discovered that membership involved taking an oath, and therefore the organisation was declared illegal and disbanded. In Timothy Exell's words, "the masters gained the day . . . many of them built large factories, filled them with looms and made the weavers work as journeymen under them; and many of the weavers were compelled to take their looms to the factory and pay a shameful rent for the standing of their own looms in the factory . . . ". Probably the largest mills to be built or extended at this time were Hillesley Mill, in 1826, part of which was "recently erected but not yet in use", and the biggest of the three Charfield Mills, which was built in 1829. But 1825 saw the end of extensive mill building activity in Wotton and its neighbouring villages. A few were extended, but, apart from noted exceptions, none was rebuilt.

During the 1830s, cloth production was concentrated into fewer and larger mills with more mechanisation. In 1833, the factory inspector for the West of England reported

Population of Wotton civic parish during the nineteenth century

	Wotton-under-Edge	Gloucestershire
1801	3393	250723
1811	3800	285955
1821	5004	336190
1831	5482	387398
1841	4702	431495
1851	4224	458805
1861	3673	485777
1871	3651	534646
1881	3349	572433
1891	3254	600056
1901	2979	634843

"... in the town and immediate neighbourhood of Wotton-under-Edge" there were many mills which had been totally closed for two or three years and, optimistically anticipating nineteen mills, found that "twelve have for some time been either bankrupt or have given up their manufacture". Unemployed families began to leave Wotton and, from 1831 to 1841, the population decreased by 780 people, or nearly 14 per cent, which was three times the proportion that left Stroud. People migrated to the Midlands or the North, or emigrated to America, New Zealand or Australia. A letter from an ex-Kingswood cloth worker encouraged people to emigrate to New South Wales, where he said a labourer could earn £1. 5s. 0d., but there was "not work for weavers especially", and therefore "people should be prepared to take on a rural occupation". Even by 1831, of an estimated 1,100 houses in Wotton, 128 were uninhabited. By 1832, the Austins, who had foolishly continued in the practice of supplying rural shopkeepers on extended credit terms, which served only to worsen their general financial position, had accumulated deficits to a total of £60,000.

In 1839, in Wotton, Kingswood and Wortley there were an estimated 159 handlooms housed in mills and loomshops and more than a third of these were unemployed, whilst the proportion of unemployed cottage looms would have been even greater. If one factory weaving family was fully employed in a mill, the total weekly income could have amounted to £1. 1s. 9d. that being composed of 11s. 9d. for the loomshop weaver, 7s. 0d. for his wife and 2s. 6d. for one child. Outdoor weaving families formed nearly a quarter of the population of Wotton in 1839, and a survey of 200 of these showed that the average weekly income of an employed outdoor weaving family was 9s. 7¼d. However, the average weekly expenditure (rent 1s. 3¼d., rates 1½d., candle fuel and soap 1s. 7½d., and food and clothing 6s. 6¼d.) totalled 9s. 6½d., leaving a weekly surplus of three farthings: "the outdoor weavers are undoubtedly in deep distress". The annual average rent for a cottage which housed two looms and had its own garden was £5. 0s. 0d., whilst a factory weaver paid as much as £20. 0s. 0d. for three broadlooms in a mill or £5. 0s. 0d. for two narrow looms, on top of the rent for his cottage. Therefore the higher wages paid to factory weavers did not necessarily mean that they were greatly better off. Weavers had slowly been forced into paying high rents for the privilege of working in a prison-like and soul-eroding environment, with starvation as the alternative. Timothy Exell rightly condemned the rents as "shameful rents . . . so they had rent at home and rent to pay to the master". A Parliamentary Report[4] had to admit "the convenience and profits of the factory system are advantageous to the master".

With poverty, came a growth in the number of local inns, beershops and pawnbrokers and associated crime and prostitution. In Wotton in 1823 there were thirteen inns and one brewer; in 1838, there were twelve inns and fifteen "retailers of beer"; in 1842, there were nineteen inns, twenty-seven retailers of beer and three recognised brewers. In 1838, there was one pawnshop; in 1842, there were three pawnshops; in 1856, there was one pawnshop; in 1858, there were two pawnshops and there was still one pawnshop in Wotton at least until 1863. Directory information is often inconsistent with property deeds and other documents, but helps to give more idea of the industrial situation in Wotton: in 1840, there were nearly twenty mills in the district and, by 1850, only half of these were still producing cloth. Pigot's *Directory* (1822-3) lists fifteen mills and three dyehouses; Robson (1837-9) lists seven mills; Pigot (1842) lists fifteen woollen cloth manufacturers and four dyers and a "teazle dealer" and notes that Hack Mill was a paper mill at that time; Kelly (1856) lists just two dyers and one teazle dealer; Slater (1858) lists four mills — Park, Charfield, Nind and Monks, and four dyers; Kelly (1863) lists two cloth manufacturers and three dyers.

Parts of an 1854 *Report on the Sanitary Conditions of Wotton-under-Edge* further illustrates aspects of the decline of the woollen cloth trade in Wotton. It claims that land values had "fallen off by a half" since 1825 and illustrates this quantitatively with the case of William Woodward[5] who owned thirty houses whose rents "since 1825" had dropped from £11. 0s. 0d. to £4. 10s 0d. by 1854. Listing three census figures, 1831 — 5700; 1841 — 4702; 1851 — 4220, the document correctly asserts "there has been constant falling off of population for some years past which is probably attributable to the decrease of the trade of the place" and "although birth rate is greater than death rate, the population has been falling off at the rate of 50 per annum for many years". Finally, (and reinforcing our previous conclusions) it states that the woollen cloth trade in Wotton-under-Edge was "best about 1813" and there was a "sudden decline" in 1825.

Beyond the 1840s the decline of the woollen cloth industry in Wotton can be traced in terms of individual mills and by 1850, there were only two mills still producing cloth — Pounds Ground Mill (now completely demolished) and Strange's Mill in Holywell. However, there was still an important concentration of mills in Kingswood and Charfield, partly attributable to the Birmingham-Bristol railway which opened with a station at Charfield in 1844. These mills included Nind, Walk, Park, Abbey, Langford, New and Charfield mills. Park Mill, New Mill and Charfield Mill were in the competent hands of the Long Family and, in 1837, Samuel Long had forseen the decrease in demand for broadcloth and introduced doeskin cloth, (requiring highly skilled weaving techniques) and he employed nearly one hundred people in the production of this cloth.

In 1854, employment was "quite good" and probably the remaining mills in Kingswood and Charfield, Monks Mill in Alderley and the dyeworks in Wotton (Strange's Mill and

Dyehouse Mill) provided enough employment for a grossly diminished population. But in 1867, Monks Mill closed down and New Mills followed in the 1870's. Park Mill closed in the 1880s, then Charfield Mill closed in the early 1890s and ultimately, Nind Mill failed in 1897.

Through increased mechanisation and efficiency, the Gloucestershire woollen cloth industry contracted into fewer and fewer mills to meet smaller demand, whilst many investors discovered that quicker and easier profits could be made in other industries or in land or finance. In Wotton, mills decayed and were demolished or, more fortunately, were used for a variety of other industries, including silk textile manufacture, elastic manufacture, printing and engineering.

Adverse economic climates, national and international competition, shortage of capital, appalling industrial relations and the advent of industrial diversification, all determined that the woollen cloth industry in Wotton-under-Edge and its neighbouring villages of Charfield, Kingswood and Wortley was unable to survive the hard realities of the nineteenth century.

Notes

1. Introduced into Wotton from at least 1788 and woven with warp thread of coarser texture than abb thread.
2. Made almost entirely of Spanish wool and dyed 'in the wool'.
3. In fact, the price of bread was the main political preoccupation of wage earners during the 1789 French Revolution, so this point is most relevant.
4. *Parliamentary Report on the Condition of Handloom Weavers*, London, 1839, from which the analysis of wages and rents is also taken.
5. Founder of the Oliver Memorial Chapel, Synwell.

CHAPTER 4
Mills

Apart from water mills and steam mills, there was a variety of other industrial buildings involved in the processes of woollen cloth manufacture. These included workshops, or loomshops, in Symn Lane, Haw Street, Bear Street, the High Street (workshops here were owned by the Austins), and in Synwell. There was a loomshop and weaving cottages at Dudley Mill, dyehouses at Potters Pond, scouring houses in Coombe and a dyehouse adjacent to the Grist Mill (which was solely a grist mill) at Coombe Lakes. Most of these buildings have been demolished and, without them, it is difficult to fully understand the organisation and scale of the woollen cloth industry in Wotton.

In fact, of nearly thirty local cloth mills which were operational during the early nineteenth century, only just less than half have escaped major demolition. Therefore, no matter how many facts, descriptions and photographs may be produced, the scale of the local woollen cloth industry with respect to the extent and variety of industrial building will never really be appreciated . . . extent — in terms of overall distribution and density; and variety — in terms of siting, size, composition, proportion, materials, construction and context, character and reputation. All of these, of course, are irretrievably lost when a building — any building — is demolished.

(I) THE KILCOT VALLEY

Hillesley Mill ST 770 905

Probably dating from at least the early seventeenth century, Hillesley Mill was worked by the Austins in the early nineteenth century, when water power at the site was supplemented by a steam engine.

The building now serves as a private residence, and most of the proportions of the industrial fenestration have been changed, though perhaps not for the worse. The trivial and opposing extensions ooze a high degree of insensitivity — merely creating space to fill, rather than fulfilling a need for more space. Their poor design is reflected in an obsequious payment of lip-service to local materials and to a vernacular which has been embarrassingly misunderstood. More courageously, the stonework of the original building has been in-filled with red brick and the informality of this proves most attractive.

New Mills ST 776 903

During the eighteenth century, this mill was owned by the Larton family. In 1802, the site was extensively developed and became a massive industrial complex; in doing so it was one of the first mills in Gloucestershire to house hand-looms and thence commands an extremely important status in terms of the Industrial Revolution. By 1839, the Austin family had acquired and expanded the premises, and in that year reported to the Parliamentary Commissioner their ownership of fifty-nine hand looms, thirty-two of which were unemployed.

An early photograph of New Mills shows a large, main factory block of three storeys and heavy dormers set into the roof. Unfortunately, most of the mill has been demolished and only a disappointingly small section of a weaving shop now remains. This is built in stone with brick dressings, and is roofed with corrugated asbestos-cement panels. Parts of the intricate watercourses at the site served a small grist mill.

Hillesley Mill, east front.

Hillesley Mill.

Alderley New Mills c.1900.

Alderley New Mills.

(II) OZLEWORTH AND WORTLEY
Hill, Hell or Ell Mill   ST 783 919

In the late seventeenth century, this mill was both a fulling mill and a grist mill and was sold in the early eighteenth century for £1,200, indicating that it was by then a large mill. This is substantiated by some recent excavations carried out by its owner. In 1825, two men stole £150 worth of cloth from the mill and each received a fourteen year jail sentence for their trouble. Cloth production ceased in 1844.

The various names of the mill give rise to special interest. *Hill* no doubt derives from the local terrain; *Hell* apparently was in reference to the quality of some of the girls and women who worked at the mill; whilst *Ell* is either a local corruption of *Hell* or refers to a particular width of cloth (an English ell-width is 1¼ yards) the production of which may have been a speciality of the mill.

All that remains of the mill is a small section of a workshop built in random rubble stonework. The later cottage is of coursed rubble stonework with large quoin stones and was probably built with material from the mill. It is roofed in Cotswold stone tiles and has brick segment-arched headed windows and door.

Knowle's Mill   ST 778 914

This mill dates from at least the late seventeenth century, and at that time belonged to the Knowle family. The mill housed two fulling mills and there was also a mill-house at the site. Records of cloth production end before the middle of the nineteenth century.

There are only one or two decayed walls of rubble stone at the site and some watercourses leading to a by-pass sluice. An early photograph gives a good indication of the original size of the building.

Hill, Hell or Ell Mill.

The Ozleworth Valley.

Knowles Mill c.1940.

The ruins of Knowles Mill.

Monks Mill
ST 772 914

At the time of Domesday (1086), Monks Mill was a grist mill, and a little later was granted to Kingswood Abbey by the Berkeleys. The capacity of the stream at the site ensured that the mill was destined for cloth manufacture, which began in the early fifteenth century, when the mill was still an Abbey mill. The mill was surrendered by the Abbey upon Dissolution in 1546. In 1613, it was substantially rebuilt and extended by its owner, Christopher Purnell, one of a long line of North Nibley clothiers and landowners. In 1631, Richard Poole bought the Manor of Alderley, and the mill was subsequently bought from the Pooles by Richard Osborne in 1716. The Osbornes extended the mill through the eighteenth century and lived for a while in Wortley House (page 111). Through marriage, Samuel Yeats succeeded to the mill and in 1812 left his son, Osbourne, to manage it alone. Osbourne Yeats gave up cloth production in 1826, following the 1825 depression. In 1839 there were, according to the Parliamentary Report, fourteen handlooms at Monks Mill, of which six were unemployed. The tenants at Directly in front of the mill, can be seen two mounds at Smiths, who also worked Knowle's Mill. In 1865, there was a water powered loom at the mill, which was probably one of the few power looms to come into the district. In 1869, Smith took most of the machinery from the mill to Stonehouse, after failing to attract a new tenant.

Fortunately, a photograph of the mill was taken in about 1880 before any structural collapse and demolition. The building was based on an L-shaped plan, comprising a long range running from east to west in three sections, and an adjacent wing at the east end of this running south in two sections. Both wings of the mill housed a water wheel, and the watercourses were necessarily complicated because the mill was driven both by stream water and spring water. Directly in front of the mill, can be seen two mounds at

Monks Mill c.1880.

Water inlet at Monks Mill.

Ivy and Monks Mill.

least ten feet in height, which are probably piles of spent fullers earth.

The first two (adjacent) sections of each range are architecturally coherent enough to be of the same period, and almost certainly date from the early seventeenth century, probably being the work done by Christopher Purnell after 1613. The second sections of both ranges involved significant changes in floor levels, and the second section of the longer range had considerably higher eaves and ridge levels, and was set back from the first section. These two were probably the lateral extensions, dating from the early eighteenth century and the beginning of the period of Osborne ownership. All these four sections had fine sets of dormer windows, effectively breaking up the scale of the whole composition. The third section of the east-west range had no dormer fenestration and certainly looks of a later period, in which case it was the Osborne extension of the late eighteenth century. All the windows in the mill were of a three-light pattern, some segment-arch headed and others flat-arch headed. The whole building was constructed of Cotswold limestone and roofed with stone tiles, thus completing what was an almost exquisite industrial building of the vernacular tradition.

Apart from some walls of the eastern corner of the main range and sections of the smaller wing, the building has been demolished. The site, however, makes an interesting, if sad, visit and affords some constructional details, but everything is thickly overgrown and its current use as a haunt for goats seems cruelly to deride its former prosperity and beauty.

Penley's Mill ST 769 913

Little is known of this mill, but it dates from at least the mid-sixteenth century. After a series of tenants, it was leased to Daniel Adey of Wotton in 1708 and, by 1800, John Penley was the tenant. The mill housed a fulling mill, and there was also a dyehouse at the site. John Penley's son succeeded to the mill and probably continued it as a dyehouse, until shortly before his death in 1858. All that remains at the site is a small out-building, some iron sluice gates and a hopelessly over-restored cottage.

Broadbridge Mill   ST 967 913

Just a little further down stream from Penley's Mill, and within view from the Wortley-Alderley road, is Broadbridge Mill. In the mid-sixteenth century it was known as *Wortley Mill* and later the tenancy passed to the Poyntz family (see Newark Park, page 100). In 1631, Richard Poole bought the mill as part of the Alderley estate (which included Monks Mill), and at that time it was a double mill, housing a grist mill and a fulling mill, with an adjoining mill house. In 1798 it had two fulling stocks and a gig-mill and was probably powered by one high-breast wheel. In 1827 the mill was solely a grist mill, and whether it manufactured cloth again before its closure during the 1840s is doubtful.

The building became a saw mill and in the late 1960s was converted for domestic use: because of this, much of the original fenestration has been altered, especially on the north side, (see Appendix I). The mill is of three storeys, constructed in stone, with stone tiles on the south pitch of the roof and concrete tiles on the north pitch. It conforms to the by-pass pattern, with sluice gates still intact on the north side of the mill. Water feeds into the mill through a large brick-arched inlet, but the wheel has been removed.

Grindstone Mill   ST 764 913

At the beginning of the seventeenth century, this mill belonged to the Poyntz family and, by 1650, was a multifunctional mill, housing a smith's forge, a grist mill and a fulling mill, all under one roof. There was also a dyehouse at the site. In the early nineteenth century, it was owned by the Austins, who probably used it for cloth milling. In one of the adjacent fields there were cloth drying racks.

Broadbridge Mill, east.

Broadbridge Mill, west.

Grindstone Mill.

Judging by the size and style of the mill, it did not undergo the transition to the factory system and must have continued on the putting-out system until its closure. The small building is of two storeys constructed in rubble stonework and now roofed with Welsh slates. The pond has been filled in, but the brick-arched inlet is plainly visible and is positioned in the side of the mill house, so that the water wheel was in the basement of the house. Inside the mill, the position of the wheel (under the house) is clear, but the wheel itself has been removed.

The very pleasant mill house adjoins the mill and gives a good idea of the domestic accommodation of a small fulling mill. It probably dates from the late eighteenth century or early nineteenth century. The house is built of squared rubble stonework brought to courses; it has nicely scaled quoin stones and is roofed with stone tiles. The two gabled dormers and the main gables are topped with copings. All the windows have two-light casements and mitred stone surrounds with stone mullions. Each window and the door has a hood mould — a functional and traditional detail to throw water away from openings.

(III) KINGSWOOD, CHARFIELD AND HUNTINGFORD

Nind Mill ST 755 915

As an Abbey Mill, Nind Mill has a history of several centuries, but is not as well documented as Monks Mill. After the Dissolution, the Mill belonged to Sir John Thynne of Longleat, and by 1612 it was in the hands of the Blagden family, and remained so for six successive generations. In 1738, the property was decribed as a 'fulling mill and other mills', and in 1808, as a 'fulling mill, gig mill and other mills and a mill house'. In 1817, the tenancy was shared, but some of the mill was retained by the Blagdens. In 1818, a newly

Nind Mill c.1910.

Nind Mill.

erected part of the mill had two water wheels and was occupied by new tenants. The mill took advantage of a convergence of copious springs and streams, but it was not as important as Monks Mill until at least 1825. Sections of the mill being used at about that time probably dated from the eighteenth century, and before. In 1834, the mill generated about 20 horse power, but there was often too much water in winter or too little in summer. By 1839, Messrs Council & Co. had twenty handlooms at the mill, but ten were unemployed. Messrs. Millman, Hunt & Co. were producing woollen cloth in 1894, but after 1897 Nind Mill turned to flockwork and thence became known as 'The Rag Mill'. In 1907, Messrs Millman, Hunt & Co. were "fortunate in their supply of water power, which is sufficient to drive three large water wheels" and some parts of their mill had "been in use for three centuries".

In the nineteen sixties, Nind Mill was almost entirely demolished. It comprised a large, five storey block attached to a four storey L-shaped block; and these main ranges included dormer windows set into deep, hipped roofs. On single and two storey layouts surrounding the mill, there were various workshops, stores, scouring sheds, and a dyehouse and several mill cottages. As previously mentioned, the reservoir was one of the largest and most expensive in Gloucestershire and, although now dry, its outline is discernable. The whole complex had more in common with North Country cotton textile mills than with Gloucestershire woollen cloth mills, but nevertheless it was still extremely well built and detailed, and very attractive. A visit to the site gives only the merest hint of its former size and prosperity as a woollen cloth mill, and indeed, this scale and effectiveness of destruction is very disturbing.

Walk Mill ST 750 919

This mill was also an Abbey Mill. The name suggests it was a fulling mill when fulling a cloth was done by treading, or

Walk Mill and later Mill House.

Park Mill.

Detail of Park Mill warehouse.

Park Mill warehouse.

'walking', that is, before the thirteenth century. In 1764, part of the mill was involved in flockwork. It seems that most of the site was completely rebuilt about 1810, and then significantly extended about 1820, so that by 1839 the mill consisted of two main ranges of a total length of 150 feet and was powered by three wheels. Cloth production ceased at Walk Mill during the 1880's.

Much of the original mill was burnt down and only small parts, including a steam engine room and chimney, remain. An older mill house has been converted to offices, which serve the printing works now occupying the site. Nearby, former workshops with long industrial windows have been nicely converted into cottages, and behind these there are good terraces of mill-workers' cottages.

Park Mill   ST 752 921

Grouped here with the Kingswood Mills because it is situated on the outskirts of the village, Park Mill, unlike its neighbouring mills, does not lie on the Little Avon, but on a tributary which drains the Tyley Bottom and runs through Wotton to join the main stream in Kingswood.

Park Mill was an Abbey Mill originally known as "Berkemyll". Its millpond covered an area of more than an acre and, with its steep embankments, is typically medieval in character. William Long, who worked several of the bigger mills which survived into the late nineteenth century, occupied the mill in the mid-nineteenth century, and again in the 1880s, the decade during which the mill closed.

Although rather dilapidated, the mill is an interesting longitudinal building of several identifiable sections. Adjoining the mill house is a small industrial range which may have housed a gig mill; followed by a water powered fulling mill with provision for cloth drying above; and then a three storey spinning and weaving block. Next, is a double-bayed warehouse, with high, twin entrances, which have witnessed better days but are nicely arched in Flemish-bond brickwork. The last sections are partly domestic and partly industrial in character, and include some former office accommodation. On the north side of the mill is the dry mill pond and the remains of a wooden sluice which heads a short leat, leading to the fulling mill.

The whole building displays an agglomeration of stonework and brickwork and a juxtaposition of window types: some long, some narrow, some segment-headed and some flat-arch headed. The roof supports materials of equal variety — including concrete interlocking tiles, clay pantiles, Welsh slates, stone tiles and corrugated iron, which probably all serve to let the rain in. Held together with ivy, and displaying an air of 'couldn't give a damn', one can only feel a certain affection for this weathered antique, dating from the seventeenth, eighteenth and nineteenth centuries.

Kingswood Abbey Gatehouse

A brief description of the remains of Kingswood Abbey is appropriate before touring the Kingswood Mills.

The Cistercian Abbey at Kingswood was founded in 1139, and by 1220 controlled Monks Mill, Abbey Mill and Ithell's Mill. After the Dissolution of the Monasteries in 1540, much of the Abbey was demolished and the stone sold for building materials elsewhere. In about 1830, the significant remains were pulled down and some pieces found their way into local buildings; for instance, a thirteenth-century outer doorway from the Abbey was inserted into the west facade of the National School (in the Chipping), which was built in 1837.

The sixteenth-century gatehouse and some precinct walling are the last remnants of Kingswood Abbey. In the central drop-arched Gothic window is finely carved Renaissance-styled mullion. On the crown of the crocketed gable is an intact crucifix. On either side of the gateway is a pinnacled buttress, and under the gatehouse there is some attractive lierne-vaulting with nicely carved bosses.

Abbey Mill ST 746 921

Initially a grist mill, and originating at least thirty years before Monks Mill, Abbey Mill was making cloth long before 1540. In the early seventeenth century, the mill was described as being in 'a very poor condition' and by the end of the seventeenth century, the mill once more became a grist mill, and continued corn-grinding for a century until, in 1801, it was converted back to cloth manufacture. In about 1827, a small steam engine was introduced to supplement the water power, "very irregular and short in summer", which was probably supplied by two wheels. The mill was producing cloth in the 1870s, but was largely destroyed by fire in 1898.

After the fire, Abbey Mill was rebuilt on its existing single and two storey layout for the manufacture of elastic braid, under the ownership of Messrs Tubbs, Lewis & Co. At the site there is an accretion of stone, brick and corrugated iron buildings, dominated by a fine octagonal brick chimney stack.

Barely had Abbey Mill opened for elastic work, when another accident occurred: on July 21 1898, a new 'Lister' boiler exploded, killing one man and injuring four. The interesting and very detailed investigation which followed, blamed the explosion upon defective casting, and held Listers responsible for the tragedy. Incredibly, the boiler had been installed with no safety valves and no pressure gauge.

Adjacent to the Mill is a good early nineteenth-century terrace of five workers' cottages. The contemporary division of labour is directly manifested by the northerly end-terrace cottage which is bigger than the others and housed a foreman. The foreman's cottage has a fanlight above its front door. The whole terrace is of three storeys, built of stone with brick dressings, and has a Welsh slate roof.

Kingswood Abbey Gatehouse.

Abbey Mill cottages.

Fire at Abbey Mill, 1898.

Abbey Mill.

Langford Mill ST 745 924

Although perhaps older, this site is first mentioned in the late eighteenth century, when Langford Mill was a fulling mill. In 1801, the mill was owned by Humphrey Austin, but let to Thomas Mercer for an annual rent of £80. 0s. 0d. It was probably Austin's eldest son Lestrange Southgate Austin who was responsible for the complete re-building of 1822. During the 1850s the firm of Perrin & Chapman was using the mill for cloth manufacture but soon afterwards it became a silk mill and was bought by Tubbs & Lewis. It is now used for storage.

Langford Mill is a very handsome, late Georgian, factory building of four principal storeys, with lofts above and with beautifully proportioned main facades of eight window bays. On the narrow south gable face is a vertical series of five loading doors. The doors and the double-hung vertically sliding sash windows of the east and west elevations, have brick segment-arched heads. The mill sits adjacent to the stream, and seems to have been of the collateral type. It has a large, brick-arched water inlet on the east side and twin, brick-arched water outlets with stone key-stones on the downstream, west side. The building is constructed in coursed, squared rubble stonework with ashlar stone quoins and is built off foundation courses of brickwork. Set into the east facade in the middle of the second floor is an "1822" date stone and between the ground and first floors, there are three pieces of tracery or vaulting which was probably taken from the ruins of Kingswood Abbey. The roof, which is in fair condition, has small rooflights and a good covering of Cotswold stone tiles, subtly diminishing in size[1] from eaves to ridge. This reinforces a strong sense of functional stability and completes a building of unaffected, restrained attractiveness.

Langford Mill.

New Mill ST 732 932

Originally named *Sury Mill*, the origins of this mill can be traced back to Kingswood Abbey era. In the early sixteenth century, Sury Mill was a fulling mill, and in 1741 was a fulling mill and a grist mill and the property included a "Rack Close" field. In 1806, the mill and surrounding land was bought by Humphrey Austin, and then completely redeveloped and let to George Austin in 1811, by which time the mill was known as New Mill. On the site were various smaller buildings including cottages, stables, outhouses, drying stores and dyehouses. In the mill itself, were at least five water wheels capable of generating about 40 horse power to drive a variety of fulling stocks, gig-mills and other machinery. In the 1840s Lewis & Dutton (of Wotton-under-Edge) owned the mill and used it for cloth manufacture. Later, another firm used it for silk textile production, but in the 1860s woollen cloth was again produced, under the new ownership of Samuel Long which continued until after 1870, when Tubbs & Lewis bought the mill for elastic manufacture.

New Mill is a very fine piece of industrial architecture, dating from about 1810, and it is difficult not to shower it with compliments. Arranged on a north-south axis, it has six storeys, including one of dormers built into a massive hipped roof, which is set behind a low parapet and covered with Welsh slates.[2] The otherwise daunting scale of the east facade, with its eighteen bays of segment-headed windows, is reduced by extremely sensitive proportioning and by the introduction of a staircase and clock tower, which is positioned with eight bays to the north and nine to the south and is finished with a nice ogee-shaped gable. The proportions of the building are accentuated by white-painted collars of a series tie-beams which run between the floors.

The mill is uncompromisingly constructed in brick and has the merest suggestion of diaper-patterning along the east

New Mill.

Converted wool drying stove at New Mill.

elevation. On the south wall are the initials of Humphrey Austin in letters four feet high of burnt brickwork. New Mill sits very comfortably in its landscape, behind a large mill pond, and derives its beauty from forthright simplicity and honesty. It is, in short, a most superb example of early nineteenth century industrial architecture.

Among the buildings on the site which are contemporary with, or older than, the mill are some cottages, offices, single-storey dyehouses, and an excellent example of a circular wool-drying stove, which has been well incorporated into the present office accommodation. It is built in coursed, squared rubble stone and has a delightful circular roof of stone tiles, with overhanging eaves to a continuous cast-iron gutter. At the apex of the roof there is an air vent capped with a very small octagonal roof and topped at the pinnacle with a weather vane.

New Mill is listed by the Department of the Environment as a 'Grade 2' building and its present condition is a credit to its owners.

Ithell's Mill   ST 733 932

Unfortunately, nothing of this mill survives, but it stood about 600 metres downstream from New Mill and, initially an Abbey Mill, dated back almost to the early twelfth century. It was recorded in the late thirteenth century, the early sixteenth century, and passed out of Abbey control in 1545. It changed hands several times during the seventeenth century, when it was a fulling mill and a grist mill, and towards the end of the eighteenth century, Humphrey Austin owned it. During the nineteenth century, the mill became a flock mill and continued flock work until at least 1867.

Charfield Mill   ST 723 930

In the early nineteenth century, Samuel Long owned Charfield Mill. The water power amounted to nearly 50

The earliest (1812) of the Charfield Mills.

The Charfield Mills.

Date block on Charfield Mill.

horse power, but was very unpredictable and, by 1833, steam power had been introduced. In 1839, there were sixteen handlooms at the mill, operated by sixteen men and seven children, and by 1890, there were forty looms. The Long family worked the mill throughout the nineteenth century, until cloth production ceased in the 1890s.

The Charfield Mill complex consists of three mills which are totally different in character. The earliest was built in 1812, and is a clear example of a bridge-mill, with water running into the mill through twin inlets under the bridge, which carries the Charfield-Huntingford road. This mill probably housed two water wheels, and is a very solid, square, rather heavy building of four storeys and with dormers set into a high, short-ridged, Welsh-slated hipped roof. It is built of random rubble stonework and has brick segment-arched heads over the windows, which are small, almost domestic, in scale. The second mill is a two-bay, single-storey building of coursed, squared rubble stone, and now has a double-Roman clay tiled roof with long rooflights. The largest mill was built in 1829, and has four storeys and a very steeply pitched roof, with dormers. It was powered by two water wheels, but the water courses are no longer distinguishable. Constructed in squared rubble stone with, again, relatively small segment-headed windows, the mill is rather an imposing, unfussy, and strictly functional building.

Huntingford Mill ST 715 935

Little is known of the history of Huntingford Mill, but it was a "cloathing mill" when the Austins rented it from Messrs Hibbs & Daniels in 1824, and when Samuel Long owned it in the later nineteenth century. It then became a corn mill, and in the 1950s it was grinding corn, pumping water and generating electricity with its two adjacent overshot water wheels.

A datestone indicates that parts of the mill may date from

the early seventeenth century. The building is of three nicely proportioned storeys in rubble stonework, roofed with Welsh slates, and is in fine condition, with an inoffensive brickwork extension — the mill having recently been perhaps a little over-converted into a hotel and restaurant.

(IV) WOTTON-UNDER-EDGE

Holywell Mill or Strange's Mill ST 764 937

This may have been one of the mills owned by Jonathan Witchell, a wealthy clothier with varied business interests, who died in 1701, leaving an estate of just over £3,000. In the middle of the eighteenth century, Holywell Mill was a grist mill and was converted (or reconverted) for cloth manufacture by the Adey family of Coombe. In the early nineteenth century, J. and W. Strange were clothiers at the mill. They installed a 6 horse power Boulton and Watt steam engine, but delayed their payment and were threatened with legal action in August 1810. The Austins worked part of the mill in 1812, and shared use of the steam engine. In 1822, nearly two hundred people worked at the mill, which by then was powered by a 16 horse power steam engine, in addition to four water wheels generating another 30 horse power. The mill and its contents, which included spinning jennies, were sold in November, 1841, and cloth production continued until the late 1850s, after which it became a dyeworks, and continued as such until about 1880.

All that remains of what must have been a big mill complex, is a small square building of coursed stonework, situated at the bottom of Holywell Lane. Some outlines of watercourses are visible on the north side of the mill site.

Huntingford Mill.

Holywell Mill

Dyehouse Mill ST 763 936

In the seventeenth century, this mill was part of Jonathan Witchell's cloth manufacturing interests. The complete putting-out system continued here until the very end of the eighteenth century. In the 1830s, the mill was powered by water and by a 14 horse power steam engine. After the decline of the woollen cloth industry, the mill became a dyeworks, and finally closed down in the late 1870s.

The building is similar in layout to Grindstone Mill in Wortley, with a single-storey, longitudinal industrial section and an adjacent house, but with another industrial section at the rear. The mill probably dates from the late eighteenth century, with some nineteenth century additions and alterations. The early eighteenth-century house is nicely and simply proportioned, with rendered stone walls and stone-tiled roof. The pond is dry, but its outline on the north side is still obvious, and shows that the mill conformed to the by-pass pattern.

Britannia Mill or Neals' Mill ST 762 935

Edward and Thomas Neal bought buildings and land at this site from a bankrupt clothier, John Tattersall, in 1823. The mill already had a Trevithick steam engine, and the Neal brothers bought a 20 horse power Boulton and Watt engine in 1823, for which they requested an extension to their three month credit period. They bought a 50 horse power engine and a 20 horse power engine in 1825. Faced with the general financial crisis of 1825, and the cost of their own investments, they paid their weavers in 'truck', which led to a general weaving strike in Wotton and serious riots in November 1825, when sixteen men, women and children were shot (see page 40). Having mortgaged some of their property in 1825, they also borrowed £7,000, but by 1838, were so deeply in debt that the mill was sold. On January 10 1838, a "small mill" and a "large mill" were auctioned, and

Dyehouse Mill and mill house.

Britannia Mill.

on the following day supporting workshops at "Bear Lane" were also sold. Various items in the sales included twenty-nine broadlooms, waggons, "modern and improved machinery", and a quantity of "prime teazles".

The site of Neal's mill has been largely demolished, except for Britannia Mill, which could have spent only a short time as a cloth mill. Britannia Mill is an early Victorian industrial building, perhaps dating from about 1845, but with older sections and walls at the eastern end. It is square and plain with four storeys built mainly of brick, having flat-arched windows with stone keystones and voussoirs. The walls are whitewashed, and, although by no means acutely attractive, the mill is nevertheless very well maintained.

Britannia Mill is a 'Grade 3' listed building.

Cloud Mill ST 761 933

This extensive mill site, which was close to the Ram Inn, has been totally demolished. It dated from at least the eighteenth century, when it was a grist mill. By 1809, it was a cloth mill powered by one water wheel, and it continued cloth production until shortly before 1850.

The Steep Mill ST 758 933

The Austin family owned this site in 1763, but there was only a building on the frontage to the road, Ludgate Hill, at that time. The main mill building was probably erected just after 1800, for in 1802 H. and G. Austin bought a 6 horse power Boulton and Watt steam engine for the mill. An 1830 sale notice describes a large four storey mill, used variously as offices, workshops, press-shops and storage, and an adjoining steam mill with an attached engine house. Two cottages, blacksmiths' and carpenters' shops, and several other out-buildings formed part of the mill complex.

From January 1837 until June 1839 Sir Isaac Pitman used the building for his school, and then moved to Bath, where he perfected his system of shorthand. The mill was

The Steep Mill.

later used for church activities and was known as Church Mill. After a fire in the roof, one storey was removed, and the mill was then re-roofed with corrugated iron, "so unfortunate on a building so prominent in the view of the town from the east". Katharine Lady Berkeley's Grammar School used The Steep Mill, until the school premises near Kingswood were opened, in 1963. The building was later demolished and replaced by a modern Country Library construction. The industrial archaeological importance of The Steep Mill — in terms of the innovative installation of a steam engine as early as 1802 — has been fully explained (In the section on steam power, particularly page 31), and one can only mourn the loss.

Waterloo Mill ST 759 932

Celebrating the Battle of Waterloo in their own way, Austins built and christened this mill in 1815, and worked it until 1827, when it was leased to Lewis & Dutton, who were Wotton clothiers with interests in other mills. By 1840, Lewis and Dutton occupied Austins New Mills, and also manufactured cloth at Dyehouse Mill.

Waterloo Mill is situated behind the Shearman's Arm Pub, and is a three-storey building of squared and coursed rubble stonework with brick segment-arch headed windows, and is now covered in concrete interlocking tiles. At the east end of the building is an attached engine house. An 1815 date-stone is set into the south elevation, between the ground floor and the first floor. Parts of the building are empty, and several windows have been blocked up, but the western-most section has been converted for domestic accommodation.

Old Town Mill

This mill was built in 1817 to be powered by a 15 horse power steam engine. The engine was dependent on a poor water supply from a well and this proved to be a continuous

Waterloo Mill.

Date block on Waterloo Mill.

problem. In 1825 broadcloth and kerseymere cloth were manufactured; with steam power applied to spinning and finishing processes, but not to weaving. The mill employed two hundred people.

Old Town Mill is a very important example of a steam mill, and becomes more significant because, of the other two steam mills in Wotton, The Steep Mill has been demolished and Waterloo Mill is in a dilapidated state. Having been converted for domestic accommodation, Old Town Mill is in good condition and apart from some altered ground floor windows it has retained its original external form. The three storey building is constructed in rubble stonework and has stone segment-arched headed windows and an '1817' date stone set over the fanlight of one of the doors.

Hack Mill ST

Hakemill dates from at least 1537, when a passing reference to it occurs in a Kingswood Abbey document. Whether it was a grist mill or a fulling mill at that time is not known. However, the mill does have a later history as a paper mill, and even then had a close connection with the woollen cloth trade, because it produced wrapping papers — "sugar loaf blue and brown papers", and "best press papers for clothiers". Press papers were resilient, glazed papers which were placed between the folds of newly finished cloth to be pressed under heavy iron presses. In 1840, these papers, at one shilling each, were expensive, but lasted for several years. The position of Hack Mill, receiving all the town waste and dye pollution in the stream, rendered it totally unsuitable for the manufacture of finer paper. From the eighteenth century, the function of Hack Mill alternated between paper production and woollen cloth production. In 1773, a partnership dissolved and one partner continued until his bankruptcy in 1774. Under new ownership, paper manufacturing continued into the 1790s, and then the mill

Old Town Mill.

Hack Mill.

was converted into a cloth mill, but may have been concurrently involved in paper manufacture. Some contents of the mill were insured in 1823, and this covered carding machinery and quantities of raw wool, and although not mentioned in the insurance policy, it is most likely that the mill housed fulling stocks too. By 1842, Hack Mill was again fully devoted to paper making and was listed as such in Pigot's *Directory* of that year; and its last reference as a paper mill was in 1847.

Hack Mill is a three-storey stone building, with brick segment-headed windows and tie beams. The north and south walls are of squared rubble stonework, tied into what appear to be older, random rubble stone, gable-end walls. Now roofed in corrugated asbestos sheets, the mill is in poor condition, serving as a workshop in a scrap-metal business. Because of its history as a paper mill, it would be most unfortunate if Hack Mill was demolished, in a frenzy of prejudice against scrap dealers and untidy (but perfectly harmless) buildings.

Dudley Mill   ST 758 924

The Rev. Rowland Hill (1744-1833) built this mill, which has been totally demolished, just downstream from Hack Mill, occupying the site of the old sewage works at the end of Water Lane. The mill employed poor people (selected by Hill) and after a series of lessees, which included Samuel Long of Charfield, cloth manufacture ceased about 1845. Rowland Hill built the original Tabernacle Church in 1783, which was superseded in 1851 by the existing Victorian, Early English style church. He also financed the building of a terrace of almshouses, set beyond the Tabernacle. These are in an interesting Gothic style and were superseded on a different site by the Victorian Tudor almshouses which stand at the top of Tabernacle Pitch.

Notes to Chapter Four

1 Each region, or even each stone-tiler, had their own tile-size naming convention, ranging, for example, from the larger *long and short sixteens* and *long and short twelves* through the *short wivots*, *long and short bachelors* and the *muffett, long and short cuttings* to the *long, middle and short cocks* of the ridge.
2 As with Cotswold stone tiles, Welsh slate quarries also employed their own size-naming convention. From large *Princesses, Duchesses* and *Marchionesses*, they ranged through the *Viscountesses* and *Broad Ladies*, to the smaller *Narrow Ladies* and *Small Doubles*.

Tyley Bottom.

CHAPTER 5

Cottages

Until the breakdown of the putting-out system through the process of industrialisation and the development of factories, the local woollen cloth industry was dependent upon carding, spinning and weaving, performed as cottage industries. The factor which could determine the planning and orientation of a cottage was weaving. Cottage or outdoor weaving continued, despite the growth of loomshops, beyond the mid-nineteenth century, and many local cottages contained one or two handlooms housed in spare rooms and extensions, sometimes lit by slightly larger windows; or in attic rooms, lit by dormers. There are several, more obvious, examples of weaving cottages in Coombe Village and in Coombe Road.

A terrace in Coombe Village is on a curved plan to follow the road, and negotiates a steep bank, allowing two storeys to the road and three to the garden (south) side. These pleasant cottages are of rubble stonework with Welsh slated roofs, and each has a weaving room located on the third floor, facing south.

An attractive terrace in Coombe Road probably dates from the early eighteenth century. It has gabled dormer windows (to below eaves level) and is stone built with rough-

Weaving cottages at Coombe village (south side).

Weaving cottages in Coombe village (north side).

Weaving cottages at Coombe village.

Weaving terrace on Coombe road.

cast rendering, and is now roofed with Double-Roman clay tiles.

The majority of cottages were probably found suitable to house a handloom and were not specifically designed for the purpose, but one terrace that certainly was stands in Bradley Green, a hamlet on the southern outskirts of Wotton-under-Edge. These cottages call for very special attention. They are early nineteenth century, built in coursed, squared rubble stonework, with brick segment-headed windows with stone keystones, and are now variously roofed with concrete interlocking tiles, Welsh slates and stone tiles. The terrace is aligned on an east-west axis, and adjoins older agricultural buildings to the east. At first glance the row seems ordinary enough. However, under three roofs there are four cottages, and each has a large weaving-room which would have been suitable for two broadlooms. The weaving-rooms are lit on the north and south elevations by pairs of windows. The first end-terrace cottage has very minimal domestic accommodation and a weaving-room on the ground floor. The next cottage is a reflection of the first and has similar domestic accommodation, but its weaving-room is above that of the first cottage. This cross-over arrangement is repeated in the other two cottages and forms a rare and most interesting, if cramped, solution to a combined domestic and industrial functional problem.

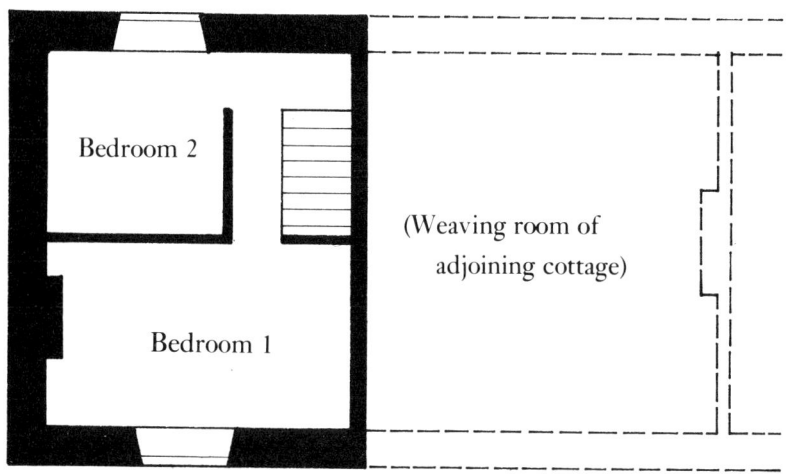

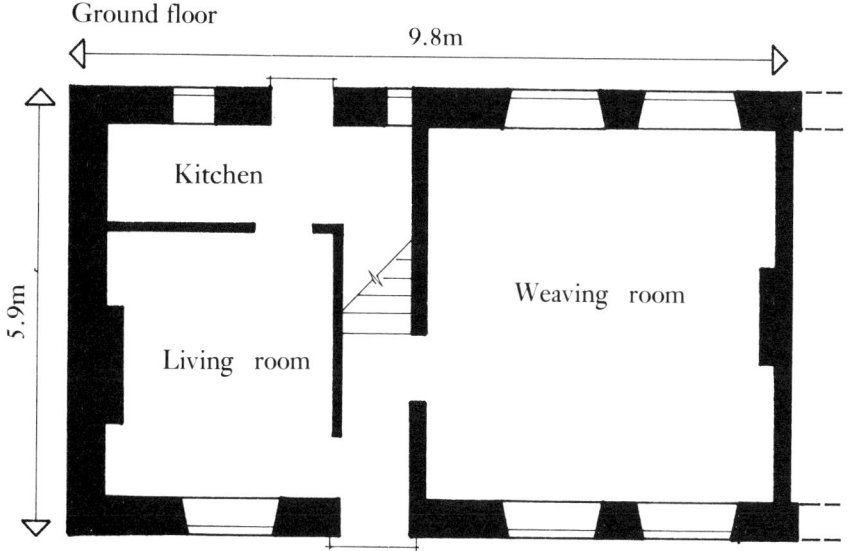

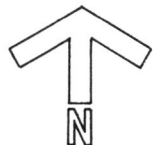

Weaving cottage in Bradley Green
scale 1:100

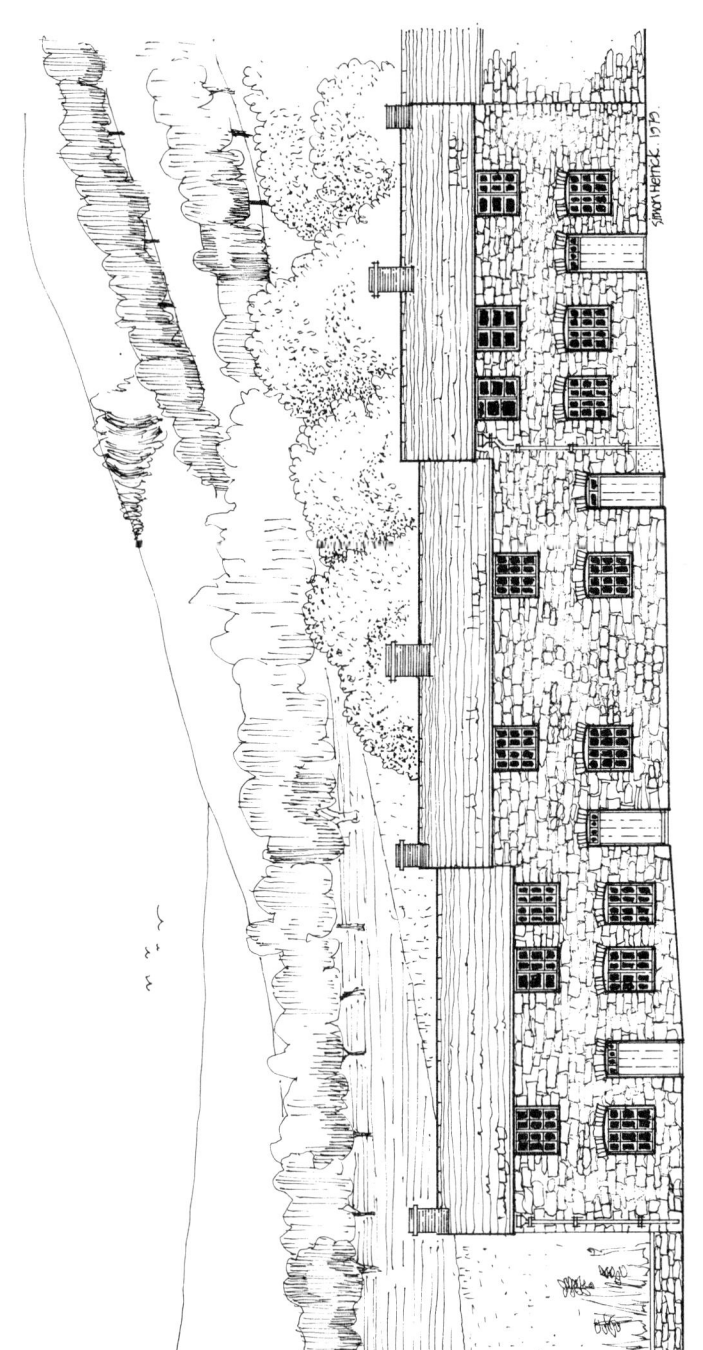

Bradley Green weaving cottages.

CHAPTER 6

Houses

Clothiers of the Gloucestershire woollen cloth industry collectively represented a wide range of wealth and prosperity. They varied from weavers who owned more than two looms and employed labour; lesser clothiers who rented or owned a mill; to those who, like the Austins, owned and worked several mills, and became entrepreneurs.

Clothiers' houses were similarly diverse in nature and size. Some more modest mill houses have already been described, but the following discussion focuses upon five larger houses which belonged to wealthier clothing families. The houses have been chosen for their very significant architectural interest, and also because their more extensive deeds and other records have allowed respective relationships between houses and families to be satisfactorily established. Newark Park, Under-the-Hill, Wortley House and The Warren are all very much alive, and as vibrant as ever. Unfortunately The Ridge has been demolished, although its architectural importance will become apparent in its obituary.

The five houses can be summarized by architectural period as follows:

Newark Park (Ozleworth)
Mid sixteenth century, seventeenth century, late eighteenth

century and late nineteenth century.
General character — eclectic!

Under-the-Hill House (Wotton-under-Edge)
Early seventeenth century, though predominantly early eighteenth century.
General character — early Georgian.

Wortley House (Wortley)
Early seventeenth century, early eighteenth century, though predominantly late eighteenth century.
General character — mid Georgian.

The Warren House (Wotton-under-Edge)
Early nineteenth century (about 1811).
General character — very early Regency.

The Ridge House (Wotton-under-Edge)
Early nineteenth century (about 1825). Demolished 1936.
General character — neo-classical.

Newark Park, Ozleworth   ST 781 931

In 1544, Kingswood Abbey property in Ozleworth was granted by Henry VIII to Sir Nicholas Poyntz, who was of an Iron Acton family of woollen cloth exporters. The family had local cloth manufacturing interests in Broadbridge Mill and Grindstone Mill. Poyntz built the original, mid-sixteenth-century *New Work*, and recent evidence supports the tradition that he used stone and timber from Kingswood Abbey. The Poyntz family later sold the house to the Rivets, who were followed, in about 1600, by Sir Thomas Lowe, Lord Mayor of London. In 1722, the Lowes sold their much enlarged Newark Park to the Hardings, from whom it was bought by the Clutterbucks, in 1769. The Clutterbucks had been cloth manufacturers since at least 1500, and came from Frampton-on-Severn, although (perhaps) originally from Stroud. Lewis Clutterbuck (1753-1810) owed much of his wealth to previous generations of clothiers in his family; he

Newark Park.

Newark Park showing Wyatt's porch on the south front.

Newark Park, present entrance.

Newark Park, Solway's two-storey extension.

held considerable property, and was rector of Ozleworth Church (his family having acquired the advowson). It was under his direction that Newark Park was remodelled by James Wyatt. The house and estate still belonged to a branch of the Clutterbuck family in 1950, when Mrs Power-Clutterbuck gave Newark Park to the National Trust.

The original *New Work* of Sir Nicholas Poyntz, was a tall, narrow house, built in a style rather similar to that of Robert Smythson (1536-1614), who was an Elizabethan architect of major significance. The early house probably consisted of a basement and two storeys: the basement, with a kitchen and pantry, was entered from the east, through a Tudor-arched doorway which opened into a central passage. Above this, another doorway was approached by steps, to lead into the ground floor (from the present garden side), which again probably had two rooms and a central passage. Because of the height of the windows and ceilings, part of the first floor possibly served as the Great Hall, whilst on the second floor there were originally three rooms, reached by a spiral staircase. Of the mid sixteenth-century house, the east front survives. It is faced (like much of the rest of the house) in finely cut ashlar stone, and has continuous drip-moulds over stone mullioned and transomed windows, and a large bayed staircase window. The original ground floor entrance is a surprisingly well preserved example of an Elizabethan aedicule; being framed by a pediment and two columns, with fluting, cabling and Renaissance detail.

During the seventeenth century, the house was greatly enlarged by the Lowe family. The existing structure offers little clue as to the appearance of the seventeenth-century house, although it obviously incorporated the original east front. There is also some evidence of a staircase running down from what was possibly a long gallery on the first floor. Contemporary with the seventeenth-century extensions and renovations is a bell-cote on the roof, but unfortunately the recently repaired bell carries no date or maker's mark.

In about 1780, Lewis Clutterbuck commissioned James Wyatt to completely remodel Newark Park. James Wyatt (1747-1813) was arguably the most successful English architect of his time, often rivalling his contemporaries, the Adam brothers (Robert Adam, John Adam, and James Adam), and succeeding Sir William Chambers as Surveyor General in 1796. His reputation is now based on his neo-Gothic self-indulgences, the best of which have been demolished. Among his more important surviving houses are Heaton (1772), Heveningham (1788-99), and Dodington (1806-1813). Unfortunately, his work at Newark Park is 'undated', so it is not possible to be more precise about when it was actually carried out. Because of his vicious 'improvements' to Gothic buildings, including Salisbury and Durham cathedrals, Wyatt earned the appellation "Wyatt the destroyer".

For Newark Park, James Wyatt designed a complete south elevation, with a large, three-arched Gothic porch. This south facade is buttressed, and is faced with ashlar stone. The windows have label-moulds, which are in contrast to the continuous drip moulds on, for example, the original east facade. Wyatt added a series of setback buttresses and crowned the whole house with a castellated parapet. His colonnaded hall is decorated in an Adam manner, and has oval ends with Doric columns, and a freize of bovine masks. The contemporary stone staircase has an iron balustrade, and is lit from the east by the sixteenth-century window bay. The window contains late eighteenth-century enamelled glass, with the Clutterbuck arms in a central pane — perhaps inserted when all the work had been completed.

In 1897, a square, two-storeyed wing was added to the north west side of the house by a local architect, Solway, and the work was carried out by Jotchams, of Wotton-under-Edge. This wing is also castellated, but in a more stylistic manner. The accommodation in this extension includes three ground floor rooms, one large bedroom, two bathrooms, and a staircase leading to the rest of the house.

Newark Park once had its own brewhouse, which probably stood to the east of the house, with a summer-house to the west. Unfortunately, both of the buildings were demolished during the nineteenth century. In the lower garden is a mid eighteenth-century brick orangery, adjoining a pond and facing west. It has ogee-headed windows, and once had a glass roof, but this nice little building has been sadly neglected: indeed, it has only recently been discovered under a tangled mass of vegetation. In the lower drive, there is a late eighteenth century folly, and the estate has three attractive lodges, which date from the end of the eighteenth century.

Newark Park commands very fine views across the Ozleworth Valley and beyond. Complete with ghost and peacock, it has a seemingly daunting and profound character. It is receiving due care and attention from a very capable National Trust tenant.

Under the Hill House, Wotton-under-Edge ST 759 937

William Venn, a Wotton clothier, acquired various properties from Lord Berkeley in 1611, and one of the title deeds related to a "tenement, barn and outhouses" at the present site of Under the Hill House. William Venn owned Venn's Mill (later known as Holywell Mill, or Strange's Mill) and was Mayor of Wotton in 1602. He died in 1617, and much of his property was held by members of his family until the mid eighteenth century, when it was sold to Edward Bearpacker. Bearpacker was not a clothier, but both of his sons were. One of his grand-daughters, Anne, founded the Bearpacker Almshouses in 1837, which are

Under the Hill, south front.

within view from, and to the east of, Under the Hill.

During the early nineteenth century, the house was bought by the Adey family. The family, and branches of it, were clothiers and landowners, and three times Mayors of Wotton. By the nineteenth century, they seem to have largely withdrawn from cloth manufacture in favour of land.

The Adeys were first documented in 1608, when "Morgan Adey" was described as a clothier in the military census of that year. The first (1666-1752) of a series of Daniel Adeys owned Knowles Mill in Ozleworth and worked Penley's Mill in Wortley. He married Sarah Moore, whose family name later occurred in the double-barrelled name, "Moore Adey". The second Daniel Adey bought Venn's Mill and in 1763, owned Cloud Mill. One branch of the family moved to Uley, and it was a Charles Adey of Uley who added 'Moore' to his son's name. This son, William Moore Adey, married twice, and both times into local clothing families: his first wife Sarah Larton of Alderley (1794) and his second wife was Emma Austin of Wotton (1806). William Moore Adey bought Under the Hill House probably just about the time of his marriage to Emma Austin. He was a Major in the army, and, in 1824, was Mayor of Wotton. His son (1810-1867), of the same name, inherited the house, and thence it passed to an elder brother, Anthony Adey, a solicitor, and Mayor of Wotton in 1841.

More Adey (1858-1942).

Anthony Adey's son, another William Moore Adey, inherited Under the Hill House when he was an adolescent, after his father died in about 1873. He deserves particular mention here.

William Moore Adey dropped his christian name and became known simply as 'More Adey'. He was at the heart of literary and artistic activity through the 1890s and was editor of the *Burlington Magazine* from about 1910 to 1918. A very close friend of Robert Ross (a sort of poet's impressario), his circle also included Aubrey Beardsley, (see Appendix III), Robert Graves, Osbert Sitwell, Siegfried Sassoon, and Oscar Wilde. In their autobigraphical works, Sir Osbert Sitwell and Siegfried Sassoon both gave vivid descriptions of More Adey as a totally eccentric and bizarre character. Sir Osbert Sitwell remembered him as resembling a watercolour of Lenin, as if painted by Burne-Jones. He talked incessantly about war and politics, and having taken a politically "advanced view", convinced himself he was a dangerous anarchist. The police, he liked to think, were always after him, and when speaking of a new flat in Burlington Gardens, he said, "This place has great advantages. It's convenient for the police. Whenever they want to know where I am, they can just send someone around the corner from Vine Street to look through the window". More Adey was in fact "thoroughly innocuous", but could be, at worse, a little irritating: after working late, he often arrived at number 40 Half Moon Street around two o'clock in the morning, and, thinking it was only seven o'clock in the evening, expected Ross to take him out to dinner. He believed his coveted Gold Flake cigarettes (one of the cheapest variety) were exclusively available through his landlady, whom he roused in the middle of the night, begging her for a packet. Sir Osbert Sitwell "greatly liked this intensely fantastic character", but Siegfried Sassoon treated him with a little suspicion.

Sassoon could not clearly remember More Adey's features because Adey "seemed always to shuffle about at night"; but he had an impression of a "sallow, moody little man with lustreless eyes", cropped hair and a matted, moth-eaten beard. By no means spruce, he was not far from dingy. He "smoked ceaselessly" and, although he could be humorous and even playful, he was a very solitary and frustrated man. Whimsically mysterious about himself, he thought the Government rated him as a highly dangerous "secret agent", and indeed "could have passed for one".

Adey's conversation "consisted of blurred reflections of the original" which drove Sassoon, bored by two o'clock in the morning, to a "state of suppressed yawn". Vaguely respected as an art authority and widely suspected of being dotty, the "squire from Gloucestershire" retired in about 1920 to his "fine old manor house", Under the Hill. After a short relaxed interlude, More Adey decided the house contained hidden treasure. He hired workmen, filled them with cider and, suitably intoxicated, they all set about pulling the house apart in vain search. The work was supervised by More Adey dressed in a long black cloak and carrying a tame rook on his shoulder. "The poor old Lord of the Manor was finally removed from the scene to live on for a few more years as a certified case of mental derangement". He died in 1942.

Under the Hill* house evolved through the seventeenth century from the tenement, barn and outhouses described in the Berkeley grant of 1611. The rear of the house — traditional in character, and difficult to date accurately — provides half an idea of how the original house looked, with sturdy, hipped-roofed dormer windows and fenestration of an almost industrial nature. During the early eighteenth century however, the house was extended and re-styled.

A close observation of the east (garden) facade shows that the character of the upper storey is earlier than the first two storeys: this third storey was added in 1726 and its windows have heavier glazing bars which are comtemporary with this. However, the windows of the lower two storeys have more delicate glazing bars which have a mid to late eight-

---

* It is difficult to say when the house acquired its name; perhaps after the rebuilding of 1726, or perhaps when William Moore Adey bought the house in the early nineteenth century. Its first Directory entry was in Pigot's *Directory* of 1842, when "Mrs (Major) Adey" lived at "Under the Hill". This invalidates usual opinion which holds that Beardsley gave the house its name. He borrowed the name, but did not coin it.

Under the Hill.

eenth century feel about them. These were obviously inserted as an effort to update the facade of the house, but when the work was done, the upper storey was left in its original state. This juxtaposition of window styles, therefore, does not help in accurately dating the first two storeys, but the upper storey is contemporary with the roof turret, which contains a bell dated 1726.

What was probably a simple portico, with perhaps pilasters supporting a pediment, or perhaps a plain cantilevered hood over the front door, has foolishly been removed — possibly by More Adey. The (otherwise handsome) east front has double-hung, vertically sliding sash windows, and a continuous string-course between the first and second floors, and a fine dentil-moulded cornice at the eaves. The hipped roof has two dormer windows, whose eaves are excellently detailed with moulded cornices. The house is mainly of rubble stonework, rendered with colour-washed, rough-cast and roofed with stone tiles. Inside the house, some attractive oak panelling must have escaped More Adey's notice.

Wortley House, Wortley　　　　　　　ST 766 917

Richard Osborne, a clothier and Mayor of Wotton, obtained the first of his series of leases of Wortley House in 1703. In 1716 he bought Monks Mill, having previously rented it, and in the same year Wortley House was described as "new erected" by him, so he had by then probably extended the original house which dated from at least the mid seventeenth century. Richard Osborne's son, of the same name, succeeded to the house and the mill, when his father died. A grandson, John, was the last of the male line, and he lived in Wortley House just after the mid eighteenth century, though he later moved to Monks Mill House (close to Monks Mill, but now demolished). Mainly through wealth generated by Monks Mill, the Osbornes invested in land at Kilcott, Tresham, Wickwar and Wortley: John Osborne's inheritance included 450 acres of land, eleven houses and five mills; but only Monks Mill can be identified as one of these five mills.

Wortley House was enlarged and remodelled in its present form in 1771, perhaps in preparation for the marriage of John Osborne's eldest daughter to Samuel Yeats, in the following year. However, Samuel Yeats and his wife do not seem to have lived in the house, and it was offered on lease in February 1776, and subsequently let to a small-scale clothier. Samuel Yeats took over Monks Mill in about 1795 and formed a partnership with his son, Osborne Yeats. In 1800 Osborne Yeats married and settled at Wortley House. In 1812 Samuel Yeats retired and left his son to manage the mill alone. But Osborne Yeats was more interested in his shooting than in running his business. By 1826 he was bankrupt, and he autioned all his effects in Wortley House before leaving the district. Samuel Yeats came out of retirement to manage the mill for three years, until his death in 1829.

Probably the last clothier — tenant of Wortley House was John Metivier, who lived there during his tenancy of Monks Mill from 1830-34. Later tenants of the house were mainly farmers, one of whom subjected it to appalling indignities: he stored potatoes in the drawing room and kept two horses in the dining room. Fortunately, Wortley House was sensitively restored in 1926.

Although Wortley House dates from at least 1649 (when its first identifiable record occurs), the existing house owes little to the seventeenth century, other than a detached, single-storey wing at the rear, which at one end has eaves only just above the high ground level. Wortley House was given its present, mid-Georgian appearance, almost certainly in 1771, which is the date of a plumber's mark, stamped into the lead guttering. The house is finished in colour-washed, rough-cast render, and is constructed mainly of random rubble stone laid in mud mortar, whilst the second floor facade is of local soft bricks.

The convincingly proportioned front elevation has double-hung sash windows, unsymmetrically grouped in two and three bays, with continuous drip-moulds over, and a dentil-moulded cornice at the eaves. The six-panelled front door with a fanlight is flanked by two columns, with a pediment which awkwardly projects above the sill of a first floor window. This modest portico probably replaced a plain, cantilevered porch. The small lean-to, attached to the east of house, was built as a servants' outdoor water closet, probably during the early nineteenth century.

Inside the house, and dating from the early seventeenth century, is a fine, open (square) staircase, with barley-sugar balusters. The staircase is lit by a large (and rather incongruous), ten feet square Venetian window, which still has plenty of its original, six-by-four inch, green panes.

The Warren House, Wotton-under-Edge ST 766 933

The Austin family was involved in the woollen cloth industry for two hundred years, and by the nineteenth century had become the most prominent clothing family in Wotton-under-Edge. Edward Austin (1634-1708) was one of the earliest of the line, and he, like most of his descendents, was a clothier. The Austins held mayoral office more times — eighteen — than any other Wotton family, and Edward Austin's son, John, was the first to do so. John was a clothier, and a friend of Richard Osborne, of Monks Mill and Wortley House. It was John Austin's grandson, Humphrey Austin (1747-1829), who rose as the most salient in the Austin ranks. He was known as Great Humphrey, and his extensive activities — renting, letting, building, buying and selling mills — suggest that he virtually lived, breathed and died woollen cloth industry. It is surprising that he found time to fulfil his civic duties during his two

The Warren House.

terms as mayor, in 1784 and 1800. To his initiative we owe one of the finest pieces of industrial architecture in Gloucestershire — New Mills, at Kingswood. Humphrey Austin's brother, William (1742-1827), departed from the Austin norm by following a distinguished academic career, whilst Humphrey worked with a lesser partner, George, to whom he was not directly related. A cousin, Edward Austin, was also a clothier, and in 1820 was living in a house at The Chipping, whilst another, Edward Austin, built the core of Ellerncroft House, in 1823. The several Austin partnerships were run as family businesses and, variously known as 'H. and G. Austin', 'Messrs. Austin', 'Austin Bros.', and so on.

The Austins' problems were those common to the Gloucestershire woollen cloth industry: international and domestic competition, difficulties of transport and communication, and industrial relations — but were aggravated by inefficient management. Perhaps this was inherent in the family business structure. However, they survived the eighteenth century and, as we have seen, commenced the nineteenth century with great innovatory spirit. But the nineteenth century demanded bigger risks and higher stakes. When the Russian market was lost in 1807, the Austins were left red-faced, holding a mammoth stock of £15,000 worth of cloth. Furthermore, they were content to supply totally unreliable rural shopkeepers on over-generous credit terms. Like many Gloucestershire clothing families, several of the Austins withdrew capital from the woollen cloth industry, in preference to other, safer investments — especially land. By 1832, 'Austin Bros.', were insolvent and debts exceeded assets by £60,000. Although £13,000 of this was owed to the Adeys, most of the other creditors seem to have been within the family. Their cloth manufacturing interests had embraced Alderley New Mills, Hillesley Mill, Ithell's Mill, Grindstone Mill, Langford Mill, New Mills (Sury Mill), Strange's Mill, The Steep Mill,

Waterloo Mill and various workshops and dyehouses: Austins were to Wotton-under-Edge, what Ford is to Dagenham.

In 1792, Humphrey Austin bought 110 acres of wooded and agricultural land at Hentley Warren, from his friend, the Earl of Berkeley. Attached to the deeds is a map which shows there was no house on the site at that time, and although Austin may have had plans to build one, it was nearly twenty years before he did so. Apart from a close appraisal of its character, two further pieces of evidence have reinforced the conclusion that The Warren House was built in about 1810-1811: (i) Humphrey Austin retired in 1811, and (ii) a Sale Notice of 1889 states that the house was built "about eighty years ago".

Humphrey Austin died in 1829, and was succeeded at the Warren by his son, Lestrange Southgate Austin, a wealthy banker and financier. He died in 1849, during his third year as Mayor of Wotton, and left the house to his son, the Rev. John Austin, whose widow was the last of the family to live there.

The Warren House is architecturally unadventurous and yet highly sophisticated, with a restrained hint of an early Regency character. By no means the house of an extravagant, ostentatious man, it would have been very much to the taste of the old, retiring, shrewd businessman, and is most refreshing in its modesty. Nevertheless, what it lacks in architectural arrogance, it asserts by its position, secluded and aloof: it overlooks and can be seen by the whole of Wotton. This was a very powerful, symbolic reminder of Great Humphrey and perfectly expressed the contemporary relationship between employer and employee.

Carefully orientated south by south west, the house is built of stone and is finished in smooth, white-painted, stucco. Mainly of three storeys, it has three pedimented gables, with second floor Regency Gothic windows, which have intersecting tracery. The roof is covered in Welsh slates, and has a low parapet, which continues over the gables. The main entrance, of course, was originally at the front, but perhaps in order to use the entrance hall as a lounge, a small two-storey, Victorian entrance wing was added to the south east. This is similarly rendered, but is built in brickwork. The front entrance, thus redundant, was replaced by a lean-to greenhouse, some of which has been removed. This greenhouse would have been a sale feature, and the fact that it was not mentioned in a Sale Notice of 1880, but was in one of 1889, suggests that these alterations were carried out sometime during that decade: by 1889, the house had lost its "inner hall", but had gained an "adjoining greenhouse".

On 25 June 1880, the house was auctioned at the Town Hall in Wotton, and was described as "a fine old country residence". The estate included Ararat Farm (part of the original property) and "108 acres, one rood and 27 perches" of "pasture, arable and ornamental woodland". The Sale Notice of 1889 described the house (surprisingly honestly) as having a "somewhat plain exterior", and an "unfailing supply of pure water laid on throughout the house by gravitation from a spring . . . thus saving the labour of pumping". A four-roomed, "ornamental entrance lodge", noted in 1880, and in 1889, has since been demolished.

The Ridge House, Wotton-under-Edge ST 781 961

Edward Sheppard was one of the wealthiest and most influential cloth manufacturers in Gloucestershire, and inevitably became Chairman of the Clothiers Committee. His financial interests were mainly centred in Cam and Uley, but he chose to live in Wotton. In the early 1820s he commissioned George Stanley Repton (see Appendix III) to design The Ridge House, which was built on the Ridge (or Edge) estate, commanding extensive views over the Severn

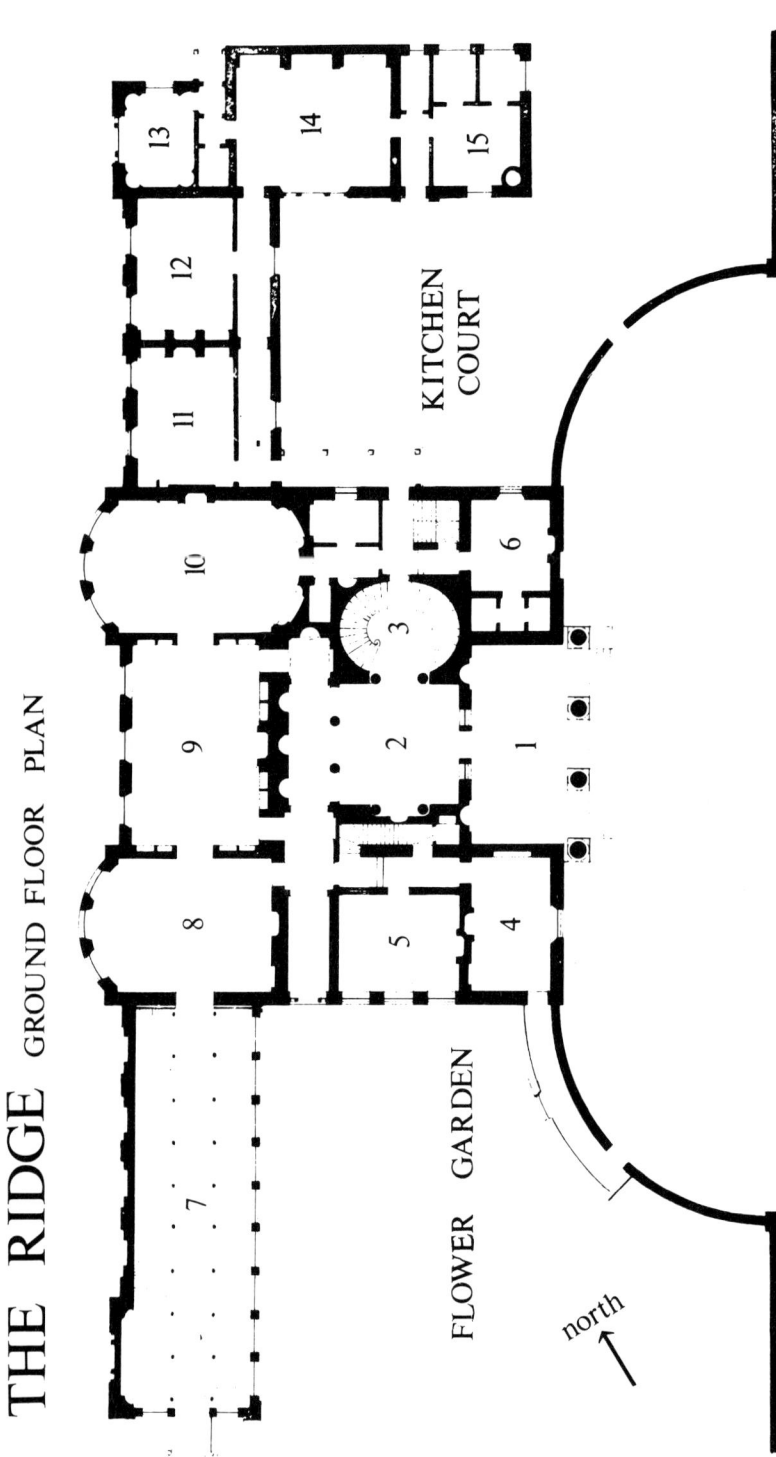

Vale and approached from the road leading from Wotton to the Dursley crossroads. Interestingly enough, Sheppard tried to breed Spanish Merino sheep at the estate, but the experiment failed rather miserably.

By 1837, Edward Sheppard was bankrupt. His mill in Uley, which had been built through the early nineteenth century at an enormous cost of £50,000, was valued at just over £500. In the same year, The Ridge was for sale and was bought by George Bengough, a Bristol banker. His son, Charles Bengough, left the house just after 1900, and it then became a country club. After this short escapade, the house failed to attract another owner and it suffered a period as an adventure playground for some of the more daring local children. After a decade of neglect, it was all but raped and murdered in 1936.

The Ridge House was of a conventional neo-classical style, with perhaps a tinge of Italianate about it, and although the use of a fully glazed conservatory was early in this context, it was not innovatory. The east, main entrance elevation had an imposing, two-storey, recessed portico with four Ionic columns and a balustraded parapet. The central, two-storey entrance was roofed with cast lead, and arranged between two, three-storey wings. Four of the windows on the entrance facade were false and were inserted to maintain symmetry and to instil proportion. A bold continuous string course, with dentils, ran between the first and second floors. The eaves were finished with a plain cornice, and roofe gables at this end of the wings were hipped. The roofs of both the wings were covered in Welsh slates.

The side elevations of the house were plain and severe, with a modest string course running between their first and second floors.

The west rear elevation was very different in character from the entrance elevation. Either side of a plain two-storey

The Ridge, entrance façade c.1925.

The Ridge, garden façade c.1925.

bay, the three-storey wings were partly bowed. These were crowned with a cornice and a balustraded parapet, which also ran across the central bay. A plain string-course ran between the ground and the first floors. The roof gables at this end of the two side wings were originally pedimented, but were later finished with totally incompatible, solid, returned parapets.

The plan of The Ridge, from the R.I.B.A. drawings collection, is not actually dated, but is water-marked 1825. An illustration of The Ridge which was published in 1824, (*Delineations of the County of Gloucester* by T. and H. Storer) was prepared from another, slightly different set of drawings, which seem to have been similar to those used to illustrate the Sale Notice of 1837. Differences in the two plans occur mainly in the design of the conservatories, and the rooms behind the principal staircase, and parts of the kitchen block. It is impossible to say which plan the house complied to — it may have had features of both.

The house, of course, was pure show, and typical of early nineteenth century nouveau riche taste. The plan was totally impractical for the day-to-day routines of living, but eminently suited to impress friends. Circulation was characteristically tedious and must have rendered the servants' lives extremely laborious. Take, for example, the relationship between the dining room and kitchen; as it was highly unfashionable to have cooking smells in the dining room, the kitchen wing (along with the kitchen staff) was set well away from it, approached through various detours and a long passage. The rather uncommon decision to have the library as a central feature was taken either because Sheppard was academic or magniloquent: probably the latter.

Of the remaining stable courtyard block, only the kitchen wing is shown on the plans, and these buildings have now been converted into an attractive residence. There are

122

also two surviving lodges which are contemporary with the house, but unfortunately the best of these has been altered. In the lower grounds is a small decaying chapel, which the Bengoughs built in 1841, and which was finally abandoned in 1950.

Although the Ridge House was extravagant, gauche and cumbersome, its loss serves to create yet one more void in the ever diminishing continuity of English architectural history.

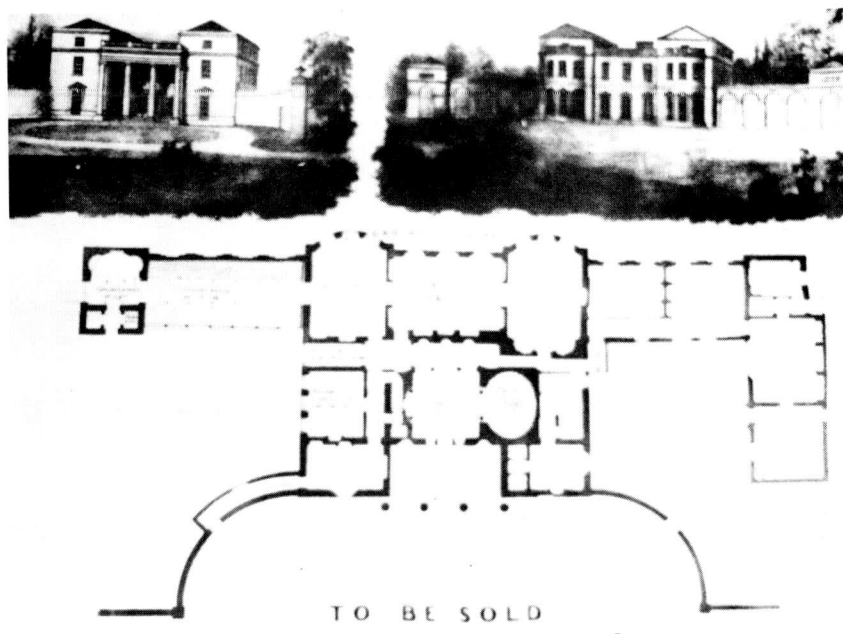

THE RIDGE SALE NOTICE 1837

"To be sold (TO BE SOLD) at the Old Bell Inn, Dursley on Thursday the 1st day of June 1837 at 10 o'clock in the forenoon.

All that capital spacious and well built Mansion House called The Ridge with the Entrance Lodge Lawns, Shrubberies, Plantations, Woods, Pleasure Grounds, Coach Houses, Stables, Garden, Conservatory, Courts and Outbuildings and the several Closes of Pasture and Arable Land all there to adjoining and belonging forming the Ridge Estate situate in the Parishes of Wottonunderedge, North Nibley, Newington Bypath and Owlpen in the county of Gloucester and lately in the possession of Edward Sheppard and containing altogether 325 Acres."

In Conclusion

The woollen cloth industry in Wotton-under-Edge created a tremendous variety of industrial and domestic architecture: surviving mills illustrate most convincingly an agreeable partnership with idyllic landscape or sensitive townscape. The majority were built with indigenous materials, but the one mammoth departure from the vernacular norm — New Mills at Kingswood — achieves its success through an uncompromising assertion balanced by a coherent juxtaposition of proportion and materials, all unashamedly assembled with confidence and guts! One looks forward to the day when an enlightened local client meets a good architect and between them is produced something of equal strength.

A special example of the result of a domestic-industrial overlap was noted at Bradley Green. The other cottages discussed were typically representative of many dotted about the vicinity. They all look so correct as to be from seeds of cotswold stone.

On the grander domestic scale, the five particular houses were as different as application of taste and fashion would determine. In at least two cases, the Ridge and the Warren, it was easy to appreciate that house and original client were compatible. One feels Sheppard at the Ridge got what he deserved, whilst the Warren somehow deserved the old, unexcited and intellectually unexciting Humphrey Austin. The Warren has a passiveness and sensitivity all of its own but the site itself must have provided 'Great Humphrey' with the last laugh on a town which virtually owed him its existence. By choosing that site he made sure he would be in symbolic command not to the day he retired but to the very day he died!

These few examples, together with all the other buildings we have discussed, contribute so greatly to the local heritage. Even buildings that are untidy or neglected can offer visual excitement, ruins offer constructional and emotional interest, but one blindly gropes for comfort when a photograph must serve as comparison and sad reminder.

The town, let's face it, is not overwhelmed with superlative buildings yet this is exactly its attraction — the rough rubbing shoulders with the smooth. But knock one down here and another there and the architectural gems shine with an absurd artificial brightness against the eroded competition. To upset the balance in this way is obviously the easiest thing in the world to do and to re-establish the balance, the most difficult. Lessons are learnt by example, and on our extremely parochial plane there are surprisingly many from which anyone who cares to appreciate buildings can learn: it is pitifully obvious that people in whose cold hands and narrow minds rest the future of local architecture, have closed their eyes.

In many ways sad to slip this study into the conservationist's lobby, I hope nevertheless that something has been learned of the town which still just manages to nestle quietly and comfortably, under the hill.

APPENDIX I

Berthold Lubetkin

The conversion of Broadbridge mill to a house is important, not because the job is particularly well done (although the interior treatment is more convincing), but because it was carried out by Berthold Lubetkin, an innovator, rather than a renovator. Born in Tiflis, Russia, in 1901, Lubetkin studied architecture in Moscow, Warsaw, Vienna and various schools of architecture in Paris, especially the Atelier Perret. Having already designed controversial and progressive buildings in Paris, he settled in London in 1930, and formed a most important group of radical architects called 'Tecton' with six graduates of the Architectural Association School of Architecture, who shared with Lubetkin a belief in architectural purity and 'functionalism'. Among the early partners were Godrey Samuel, Val Harding, Gordon Cullen, Freddy Skinner and (perhaps the more famous), Denis Lasdun, whose work includes the University of East Anglia at Norwich and the National Theatre.

Tecton's light-hearted architecture at Regent's Park Zoo, although employing highly ingenious and innovative uses of concrete, was a mere curtain raiser to 'Highpoint 1' in Highgate in 1934; which is a white, eight-storey complex of flats, arranged on a cruciform plan and whose design took considerable account of social problems and landscape. The building, quite frankly, put English architecture on the map. It embraced 'sun, sky and freedom', and conformed to Le Corbusier's concept of the point block as a component in his theoretical Radial City. In the *Architectural Review* of January 1936, Le Corbusier wrote "The building is large enough to be an example, a proof . . . an achievement of the first rank, and a milestone that will be useful to everybody". Lubetkin and Tecton's work at the Dudley Zoo and a series of London houses which soon filled English, French and American architectural magazines of the 1930s, were followed in 1938 by a rather disappointing but technically sophisticated 'Highpoint 2'. Other buildings included Finsbury Health Centre (1938), Spa Green flats (1951), and Priory Green flats (1951).

In the 1930s it had been a case of Lubetkin in London and Le Corbusier in Paris, but Lubetkin, unlike Le Corbusier, could not create a powerful and sustaining follow-through and after preparing unexecuted plans for Peterlee Newtown in 1955, he has slowly retired from practice. Although Berthold Lubetkin no longer lives there, Broadbridge Mill one day will serve as our own understated monument to this gifted intellectual and heroic architect.

APPENDIX II

Aubrey Beardsley and 'Under the Hill'.

One of More Adey's friends was Aubrey Beardsley (1872-1898), who was probably introduced to Adey by Oscar Wilde or Robert Ross. Beardsley is best known for his illustrations to Oscar Wilde's *Salome* and his involvement in *The Yellow Book*. In 1893, Beardsley drew the frontispiece for a translation by More Adey of a Norwegian play and indeed, later in the year (December) Beardsley wrote to Robert Ross inviting him and "old Adey" to Sunday tea. The first major exhibition of Beardsley's work was held at The Carfax Gallery in 1904, and was organised by Robert Ross and More Adey.

Beardsley wrote and illustrated his own poetry, and one short book, *Under the Hill*, which occupied him at various intervals throughout his brief life. The title of the book he in fact alternated, often wishing to disguise the name of its author. *Venus and Tannhanser* applied to the version which featured Venus and Chevalier Tannhauser, or sometimes the Abbé Aubrey; whilst in *Under the Hill*, Fanfreluche, a French priest, and Helen, a goddess, were the heroes. In the latter version, Beardsley's use of the 'abbé Fanfreluche' was a play on the French *abbé* and his own initials 'A.B.'. *Under the Hill* employs reference to Adey's house, and to a venereal pun — most suitable for the clouded erotic nature of the book. The first edition, published by John Lane, is now a valuable collector's item and contains five drawings: The Abbe, The Toilet of Helen, The Fruit Bearers, The Ascension of Saint Rose of Lima, and For The Third Tableau of *Das Rheingold*. Beardsley regarded The Ascension of Saint Rose of Lima as "quite one of the best of my later drawings".

"The ingratiatingly gracious and effeminately vain Fanfreluche arrived at the ombre gateway of the mysterious Hill whose pillars were fashioned in some pale stone and rose up like hymns in the praise of pleasure for from cap to base each one was carved with loving sculptures and having studied this pretty portal he passed into the underworld through shadowy corridor that ran into the bosom of the wan hill and Helen's domain.

"Helen was excrutiatingly beautiful and rather unnecessarily attended by an army of servants including her three favourite girls and her three favourite boys and dwarfs and doubtful creatures because she was adorably tall and slender and her neck and shoulders were wonderfully drawn, and the little malicious breasts were full of the irritation of loveliness that can never be entirely apprehended or even enjoyed to the utmost, whilst her arms and legs were divinely long from the hip to the knee twenty-two inches from the knee to the heel twenty-two inches as befitted a Goddess.

"Helen was quite delighted with Fanfreluche and he sat by her at supper to which had been invited hundreds of guests who were extravagantly dressed and illuminated by four thousand candles as they gorged delicious food and drank strange wines which had been cooled in buckets of snow, so that by the end of the evening, everyone was blurred and inarticulate and trying to pronounce Bassalissa and Lysistrata.

"In the morning, Fanfreluche woke at about eight o'clock, and from his pretty room, caught a peep of the sun-lit lawns outside with silver fountains and bright flowers amongst which the gardeners worked and beneath the shady trees some early breakfasters dressed for a day of hunting in the distant wooded valleys and he thought of a wonderful pair of blond trousers and of Saint Rose the well known Peruvian virgin and of 'A plea for the Domestication of the Unicorn' and attacked Wagner's *The Rheingold*"

Under the Hill gateway.

APPENDIX III

George Stanley Repton

The Architect of The Ridge, George Stanley Repton (1786-1858), was the fourth son and one of seven children of the famous landscape gardener, Humphry Repton (1752-1818). Humphry Repton followed in the generation after Lancelot 'Capability' Brown, and was a contemporary of Uvedale Price and Payne Knight, and later quarrelled with both of them. Although Humphry Repton's work was less extensive than Capability Brown's it was of a greater variety. Their ideas differed in several ways, but most obviously in the treatment of lanscape near the house and in tree plantation: Brown took lawns right up to the house, whilst Humphry Repton advocated a more subtle transition by the use of terraces or low walls; and whereas Brown planted trees in cushions or clumps on hills, Repton favoured more lavish plantation, spilling down slopes to merge with lower valleys.

Humphry Repton held what proved to be a hypocritical dislike of follies ("sham churches, sham ruins, sham bridges") but an undisguised propensity for thatched cottages, which he designed for servants or gardeners to live in. He coined the phrase "landscape gardening" (Capability Brown had used "place making") and became well known for his leather-bound 'Red Books', in which he meticulously sketched his plans for each project and obsequiously presented them to prospective clients. Through his eclecticism, Humphry Repton was able to achieve an "effective synthesis between the extremes of cosmetic artificiality and pure landscape".

He spent six very significant years with John Nash and was joined by another son, John Repton. However, the Repton-Nash partnership dissolved in 1802 after a professional misunderstanding, and Humphry and John Repton left to work together.

Just after this split, but with his father's full approval, the sixteen years old George Stanley Repton entered the office of John Nash. Nash quickly developed a strong professional and personal regard for his young apprentice. George Stanley Repton's sketch books of 1803-1805 (deposited at the RIBA library) show him, at an early age, to have been of versatile architectural talent. It was through George Stanley Repton that the extremely important Reptonian influence continued to be exerted upon Nash. This influence was felt in part of the landscape at the Brighton Pavilion (1815) but perhaps most prominently in the plans for Regent's Park, submitted for competition in 1810, and now, of course, regarded as John Nash's greatest work, although their picturesque combination of both freedom and dignity was very much a Reptonian trait. George Stanley Repton continued in practice with Nash, but he also worked with his father and brothers. In fact, his brother, John Repton, ran a very successful architectural practice, winning first prize for public builings in Parliament Square, Westminster, in 1809, although his plans were not adopted.

In 1817, George Stanley Repton eloped with and married Lady Elizabeth Scott, daughter of Lord Chancellor Eldon, who was one of the chief advisers to the Prince Regent. This episode did not meet the approval of John Nash, but nevertheless, their professional collaboration and friendship continued. Then, in about 1820, George Stanley Repton formed his own architectural practice.

The commission that George Stanley Repton received from Edward Sheppard for The Ridge House, in Wotton-under-Edge, was one of his first. Others included a re-modelling of Kitley House in Devon (1820-1825); Assembly Rooms, Aberystwyth (1820); Sandgate Chapel, Kent (1822); Widworthy Court, Devon (1830); Dumbleton Hall, Gloucestershire (about 1830) and Chipping Norton Town Hall, Oxfordshire (1842).

Because of his established family and intellectual background, and his own talent and force of character, George Stanley Repton commanded the respect of, and was able to influence, one of the most famous figures in English architectural and planning history — John Nash. On leaving the Nash office, he continued an extremely successful country house practice of his own, and sad it is to say that one of George Stanley Repton's first houses — The Ridge — no longer stands.

BIBLIOGRAPHY

Gloucestershire

Sir Robert Atkyns, *The Ancient and Present State of Glostershire*, (1712)

Brewer, *Delineations of the County of Gloucester*, (1824)

Finberg, ed., *Gloucestershire Studies*, (1957)

G.B. Grounds, *Saxon Charters of Gloucestershire*

E.S. Lindley, *Wotton under Edge*, (1962)

J. de Lacey Mann, *The Cloth Industry in the West of England from 1640 to 1880*, (1971)

William Miles, *Parliamentary Report on The Condition of Handloom Weavers*, (1839)

R.B. Pugh, ed., *Victoria History of the Counties of England*, Vol X, (1907)

Thomas Rammell, *Report on the Sanitary Conditions of Wotton-under-Edge*, (1854)

S. Rudder, *A New History of Gloucestershire*, (1779)

Alfred Shorter, *Paper Mills in Gloucestershire* Trans. B.G.A.S. vol 71

John Smyth, *Men and Armour for Gloucestershire*, (1608)

John Smyth, *Memoirs of Wool*, (1747)

Margaret and Elizabeth Taite, *Concerning ye Praty Towne of Wotton-under-Edge*, (1897)

Jennifer Tann, *Gloucestershire Woollen Mills*, (1967)

Deeds, Sale Notices and papers at the Gloucester Record Office and the Gloucester City Library, including notes and letters relating to the 1825 Wotton riots, Austin family documents, accounts of the Austin Company, Osborne family documents, and census figures.

Commercial Directories:

Gell and Bradshaw — 1820
Hunt — 1849
Kelly — 1856, 1863, 1879, 1885, 1897
Morris — 1876
Pigot — 1823, 1842, 1844
Robson — 1839
Slater — 1853, 1859

Other Sources

Architectural Record — May 1937 and May 1938; Architectural Review — October 1935, January 1936, December 1936, February 1937, November 1937, and July 1955; Pencil Points (later, Progressive Architecture) — October 1936
Brigid Brophy, *Beardsley and his World*
H.M. Colwin, *Biographical Dictionary of English Architects 1660-1840*
Anthony Dale, *James Wyatt*
Edward Hyams, *Capability Brown and Humphry Repton*
John Lane, ed., *Under the Hill Aubrey Beardsley* (with Collected Poems)
Lubetkin, The essay on Berthold Lubetken was based on architectural magazine articles: *American Architect and Architecture* December 1936 and February 1937.
Maas, Duncan and Good, *The Letters of Aubrey Beardsley*
Brian Reade, *Aubrey Beardsley*
Siegfried Sassoon, *Siegfried's Journey 1916-1920*
Sir Osbert Sitwell, *Noble Essences or Courteous Revelations*
Dorothy Stroud, *Humphry Repton*

INDEX

Abbey Mill   45, 61, 64
Aberystwyth   132
Adam brothers   104
Adam, James   104
Adam, John   104
Adam, Robert   104
Adey, Anthony   40, 107
Adey, Charles   107
Adey, Daniel   57, 107
Adey family of Coombe   81
Adey, More   108-9, 111, 127
Adey, Morgan   107, 109
Alderley   45, 107
Alderley Estate   58
Alderley, manor of   54
Alderley New Mills   19, 33, 37
Almondsbury   15
America   43
Amiens, peace of   36
Ararat Farm   117
Assembly Rooms   132
Aubrey, Abbe   127
Austin Brothers   115
Austin, Edward   113, 115
Austin, Emma   107
Austin family   33, 38, 43, 47-8, 58, 80-1, 85, 87, 99, 113, 115-6
Austin, George   74, 115
Austin, Humphrey   72, 74, 77, 113, 115-6, 124
Austin, H & G   31-2, 115
Austin, John   113
Austin, Lestrange Southgate   72, 116
Austin, William   115
Austin's New Mills   87
Australia   43

Bath   85
Bear Lane   85
Bear Street   37, 47
Beardsley, Aubrey   108-9, 127-8
Bearpacker Almshouses   105
Bearpacker, Edward   105
Bengough, Charles   119
Berkeley   26, 109
Berkeley, Earl of   116
Berkeley, Lord   105
Berkeley Vale   13
Berkemyll   67
Blackwell Hall   16, 36
Blagden family   61
Boulton & Watt   31-3, 81, 83, 85
Bradley Green   96, 123
Brighton Pavilion   131
Bristol   13, 16
Britannia Mill   32, 83, 85
Broadbridge Mill   29-30, 58, 100, 125-6

Brown, Lancelot (Capability)   130
Burlington Gardens   108
Burlington Magazine   107

Cam   117
Carfax Gallery   127
Chambers, Sir William   104
Charfield   11, 20, 45-6, 61, 91
Charfield Mills   38, 41, 44, 46, 77, 80
China   37
Chipping   39-40, 115
Chipping Norton Town Hall   132
Church Mill   87
Cirencester   14
Clothiers Committee   39
Clothiers Committee, chairman   117
Cloud Mill   85, 107
Clutterbuck family   100, 103-4
Clutterbuck, Lewis   100, 104
Coombe   47
Coombe Lakes   47
Coombe Road   93
Coombe Valley   15
Cotswold Hills   13, 72
Council & Co., messrs.   64
Cromhall   15
Cullen, Gordon   125

Derrett, Edwin   40
Dodington   104
Dudley Mill   38, 47, 91
Dudley Zoo   126
Dumbleton Hall   132
Durham Cathedral   104
Dursley   16, 119
Dyehouse Mill   17, 30, 35, 46, 83, 87

East India Co.   38
Eldon, Lord Chancellor   131
Ellerncroft House   115

Exell, Timothy   37, 39, 41, 44

Fagin, Francis   41
Finsbury Health Centre   126
Filton   15
Fox, Benjamin   39
Frampton-on-Severn   100
France   36

Gloucester   13
Gloucester Journal   40
Graves, Robert   108
Grindestone Mill   58, 83, 100, 115

Hack Mill   23, 44, 89, 91
Haden George   33
Harding, Val   125
Haw Street   37, 47
Highgate   125
Hill, Rev. Rowland   91
Heaton   104
Henry VIII   100
Hentley Warren   116
Hereford   14
Heveningham   104
Hibbs & Daniels, messrs.   80
High Street   47
Hillesley Mill   33, 41, 48, 115
Hill Mill   29, 51
Holywell   32
Holywell Lane   81
Holywell Mill   19, 35, 81, 105
Home Office   41
Huntingford   61
Huntingford Mill   80

India   37-8
Iron Acton   100
Ithell's Mill   68, 77, 115

Jotchams   105

Kilcott   111
Kilcott Valley   33, 47
Kingswood   11, 20, 33, 36, 43, 45-6, 61, 67-8, 87, 115, 123
Kingswood Abbey   54, 68, 72, 74, 89, 100
Kingswood Abbey Gatehouse   68
Kingswood Mills   67-8
Kitley House   132
Knight, Payne   130
Knowle family   51
Knowle's Mill   51, 54, 107

Lane, John   128
Langford Mill   30, 38, 72, 115
Larton, Sarah   107
Lasdun, Denis   125
Leicester   14
Lewis & Dutton   74, 87
Lister, R.A. & Co.   69
Little Avon   67
London   125-6
Long family   80
Long, Samuel   45, 74, 77, 91
Long, William   67
Longleat   61
Lowe family   103
Lowe, Sir Thomas   100
Lubetkin, Berthold   125-6
Ludgate Hill   31

Mercer, Thomas   72
Metivier, John   112
Millman, Hunt & Co., messrs.   64
Monk's Mill   20, 30, 45-6, 54, 58, 61, 64, 68-9, 111-3
Moore, Sarah   107
Moscow   125

Nailsworth   20
Napoleon   38

Napoleonic Wars   37
Nash, John   131-2
National School   68
National Theatre   125
Neal, Edward & Thomas   39-40, 83
Neal, Thomas   40
Neal's Mill   32, 38, 83, 85
New Mills, Kingswood   17, 29-30, 38, 46, 48, 74, 77, 115, 123
Newark Park   58, 99-100, 103-5
Nind Mill   29, 44-6, 61, 64
North Nibley   37, 54
Norwich   125
Nottingham   31

Oil Mill   26
Old Town Mill   32, 38, 87, 89
Oliver Memorial Chapel   46n
Osborne, John   111-2
Osborne, Richard   54, 57, 111, 113
Ozleworth   99-100, 107
Ozleworth Church   103
Ozleworth Valley   29, 33, 105

Paris   125-6
Park Mill   44-6, 67
Parliament Square   131
Penley, John   57
Penley's Mill   57-8, 107
Perret, Atewer   125
Perrin & Chapman   72
Pigot's Directory   44, 91, 109
Pitman, Sir Isaac   85
Poole, Richard   54, 58
Potters Pond   47
Pounds Ground Mill   45
Poyntz family   58, 100
Poyntz, Sir Nicholas   100, 103
Price, Uvedale   130
Priory Green   126

Purnell, Christopher 54, 57

Rack Close 74
Rag Mill 64
Ram Inn 85
Regents Park 131
Regents Park Zoo 125
Repton, George Stanley 117, 130-2
Repton, Humphry 130-1
Repton, John 131
Ridge Estate 39, 99-100, 117, 119, 121-3, 130, 132
Ross, Robert 107, 127
Russia 38

St Rose 129
Salisbury Cathedral 104
Samuel, Godfrey 125
Sandgate Chapel 132
Sassoon, Siegfried 108-9
Scott, Lady Elizabeth 131
Severn, river 13
Severn Vale 117
Shearman's Arms 23, 87
Sheppard, Edward 39, 117, 119, 121, 123, 132
Sitwell, Osbert, 108
Skinner, Freddy 125
Slater's Directory 44
Smythson, Robert 103
Soho, Birmingham 31
Solway 104
Somerset 31
South America 39
Spa Green 126
Staffordshire 33
Steep Mill 31-2, 85, 87, 89, 115
Storer, T & H 121
Strange, J & W 81
Strange, William 32
Strange's Mill 17, 32, 38, 45, 81, 105, 115

Stroud 16, 20, 100
Sury Mill 74, 115
Swan Hotel 39
Symn Lane 47
Synwell 47

Tabernacle Church 91
Tabernacle Pitch 91
Tannhauser Venus & Chevalier 127
Tattersall, John 83
Tecton 125-6
Tetbury 14
Thynne, Sir John 61
Tresham 111
Trowbridge 33
Tubbs & Lewis 69, 72, 74
Tyley Bottom 67

Uley 26, 107, 117, 119
Under the Hill 99-100, 105, 107, 109, 127

Venn, William 105
Venn's Mill 105, 107
Vienna 125

Wagner 129
Walk Mill 19, 38, 45, 64, 67
Warren House 38, 99-100, 113-4, 123-4
Warsaw 125
Water Lane 91
Waterloo, battle of 87
Waterloo Mill 32, 38, 87, 89, 115
White Lion Inn 40
Wickwar 111
Widworthy Court 132
Wilde, Oscar 127
Wiltshire 31, 33
Witchell, John 35, 81, 83
Wolfe, Joseph 37, 39

Woodward, William 45
Woollen Cloth Weavers Society 37, 39
Wortley 11, 29, 43, 46, 83, 100, 107, 111
Wortley House 54, 58, 99-100, 111-3
Wotton-under-Edge 11, 13, 16-7, 19-20, 23, 26, 31-3, 35-6, 39, 41, 43, 45-7, 57, 67, 74, 81, 83, 87, 89, 96, 107, 113, 116-7, 119, 123, 132
Wyatt, James 103-4

Yeats, Samuel 54, 112
Yorkshire 33, 40

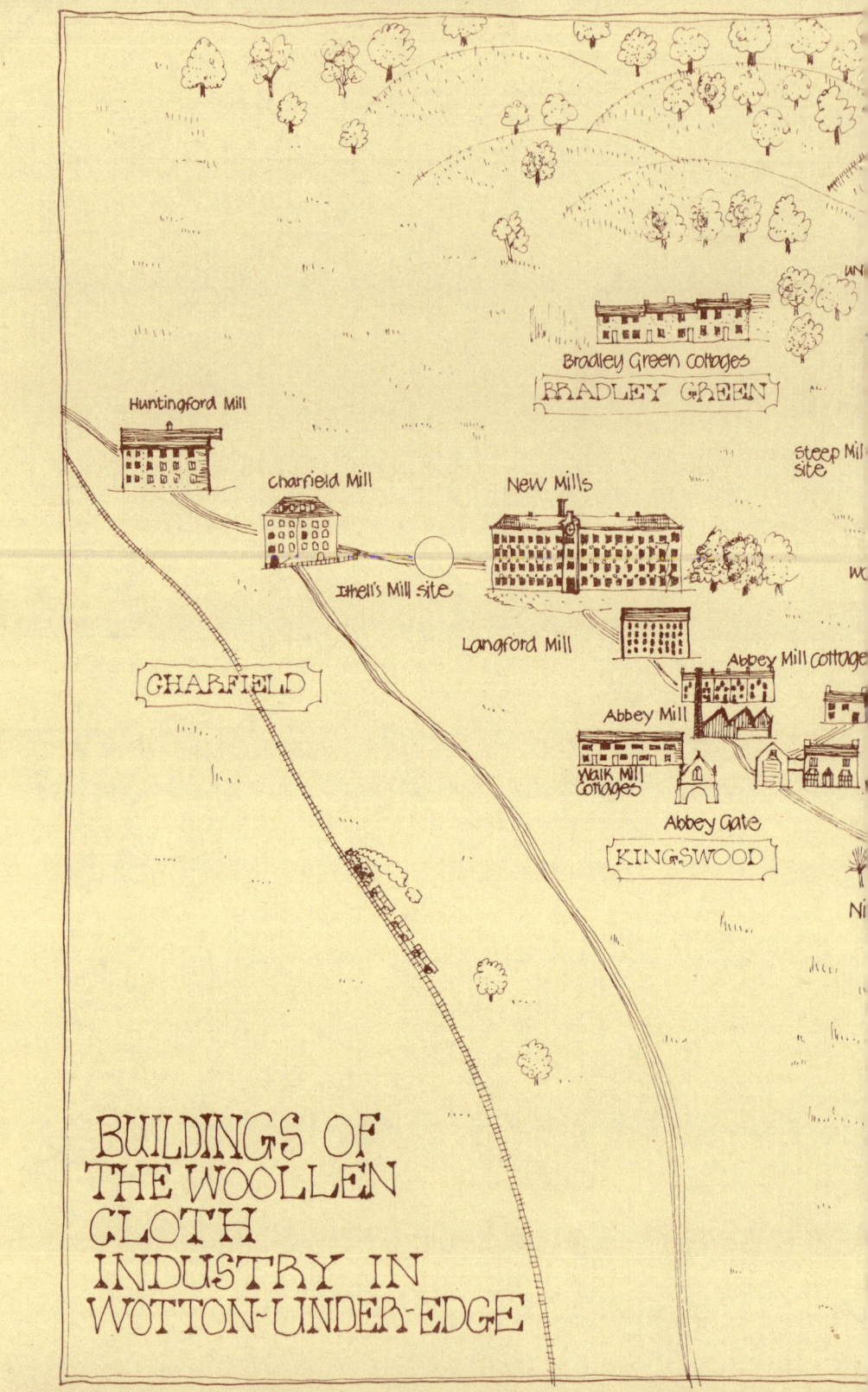